ARRIVAL PRESS

WINTER POETS

First published in Great Britain in 1992 by
ARRIVAL PRESS
3 Wulfric Square, Bretton,
Peterborough, PE3 8RF

All the poems in this book are printed on
100% recycled paper

Contents

VIII

Copy Right

I want to be a poet next year
so I'm in training now
I've written to Roger McGough
to see if he will show me how.
I'm moving up to Liverpool
to get the accent right
I'll study Merseycution
and wear my trousers tight.
I'll read about things like acid rain
and try to be profound
and practise talking in one key
I think that's how they sound.
And when I write my poetry
here comes the hardest stage
I'll
      arrange my

             words

in
   pretty

       groups to
                         take

up
    half the
             p
              a
              g
              e.

Susan Ireland

Susan Ireland lives in Dorset with her husband and young daughter. As well as being 'just a housewife' she writes poetry and dreams of being rich and famous!

Soft Shades of Night

After all the pressing cares of day
My spirit roams along the golden way
Of peaceful even, last shafts of flickering light,
Where soft breezes soothe the weary heart,
And hidden blooms their sweet perfume impart.
Gently we drift into soft shades of night.

Deeper we sink into the depths of dreams,
Lured by the ghostly, silent, luminous beams
And all pervading stillness of moonlight.
And, unknowing, smile a secret smile,
Lingering in that tranquil land awhile.
Gently we drift into soft shades of night.
   W. Turner

Wendy Turner is a member of the Havering Writers' Circle
and works in London. She has had several poems published
locally and has recently completed a volume of humorous
verse.

Earl Grey

'Early Grave' he offered.
We laughed
But not at the joke: at it's repetition.
Or was it the irony? I can't tell.
But we did,
As we did when the biscuits came round:
And so did the 'Gavin Baldie' joke.

Sitting in that unsprung chair
I shivered at fate tempted.
And took a chattering saucer
With sycophantic chirrups -

Well, this orange afternoon is not
One for morbity.
The one six months from now
Will be.

And there he sat, proud
In the heritage of small remarks
And liberal acceptance
Admiring his pseudo-lead windows;
Declaring the press of evening;
Passing judgement on family planning;
Rounding off with relevant
Shakespearian quotes.
Or was it Gilbert and Sullivan?
   Lee J. Morgan

Lee Morgan makes this first submission as a fledgling
graduate: unfortunately with time on his hands. Constructive
use of which, might hopefully lead to further publication or
a writing career.

A Small Death

It was a small death,
mourned by just a few
close family and friends.
Strange how I thought of you.

Ashes to ashes,
as dust goes to dust.
I watch my children lay you
on the cold, dark, slab of earth,
as you were once laid,
your tiny, crooked body cool as ivory.

It's been a long time now.
Strange that I thought of you.
   Peter W. Barber

Peter Barber grew up in the Channel Islands. After several years in the Merchant Navy, he now works for a major oil company on the River Humber, writing in his spare time.

My Paint Box

I open up my paint box,
With brush poised in my hand
Perhaps I'll paint a meadow
Or drifting golden sand.

Maybe a church, and blushing bride
Dressed in frothy white.
Pink carnations in her hand,
What a lovely sight.

Bridesmaids all in turquoise,
The menfolk clad in grey,
Ladies wearing every hue,
On this very special day.

No - it had better be a circus
More colours I could use,
Yellows, purples, blacks and red,
There are many I could choose.

Did you ever wonder,
That God had favourites too,
How much green there is around,
And what a heavenly blue.

Well, I'll close my paint box,
As it's far into the night.
Pictures painted in my mind,
Alas, my canvas still is white.
    P. R. Howe

Pearl Ruby Howe, known as Peggy, was born in 1929. She is married with one daughter and three grandsons. This is her first published poem and it was written to entertain clubs for the blind, over sixties and others. She has lived in Wales for 23 years.

The Human Race

Everyone's got troubles, join the human race.
Strikes, riots, drugs and war,
makes you wonder what you're living for.
Everybody out to make a dime,
rushing, slaving, got no time.
Little boxes high in the sky,
there you live, there you die.
And God looks down from a wide blue sky,
shakes his head and gives a sigh,
for the human race.

Nowhere for the children to play.
Old folk starving everyday.
Motorways stretch far and wide,
spoiling the beauty of the countryside.
Peace is very hard to find,
take your pills and blow your mind.
And God looks down from a wide blue sky,
shakes his head and gives a sigh,
for the human race.
   Anita Black

Anita Black is a pensioner, born in Yorkshire, she has lived in Hertfordshire for the past fifty years and has had several of her poems published.

Degradation and Exhortation Dec. 1976

O Britain!
Shorn of your title 'Great' by selfishness and greed,
And stretched out, sad and sick - upon the northern seas;
Sold to the Common Market, which has you on it's lead,
Dragging you down, down in slavery upon your knees.
Spurned, taunted and reviled by countries great and small,
With pains internally from fueds in family, school and
church,
On the shop-floor - and off; and rich men leaving you in
search
Of tax-free havens, - destined to bleed to death and lose
your all?

No Britain!
Rise like the Phoenix from the fire, renewed and strong,
And from the forces of disintegration free yourself.
Regain command at home and, setting right the wrong
Of sectional self-interests and personal greed for self,
Go forth in ship and 'plane across the oceans vast
And, meeting global needs with flag unfurled,
Speed on your trading-way about the world
To build once more a name more glorious and enduring than
the past.

   C. Bangham

Cecil Bangham is a retired teacher of history, living near
Ludlow. He has composed poems since 1942 - only for
personal pleasure and this is his first poem published.

Elysium

Cast loose the moorings of the mind
And sail the Sea of Thought:
Ride the winds of inspiration
'Till you find the land you sought.

All have a secret island
Of which they often dream,
Whose shores are laid with riches
Where joy and insight gleam.

The footsteps of the mighty
Lie on the sand before -
They followed their convictions
And reached that fabled shore.

But few now have the courage
To cross the ocean wide;
And steer by stars of fantasy
Against convention's tide.

Whatever fate may bring us,
Whatever lies in store;
Remember - there is always hope
Upon that distant shore.
   Susan Bullock

Sue Bullock is a zoology graduate currently serving as a
lieutenant in the WRNS. She has been writing for her own
pleasure for about eighteen months, this is her first poem
to be published.

Vagrant Art

the art of writing
is in effect a contradiction
in terms
by defining it
as an art
it becomes in the mind
of a vagrant
little more than a hobby
when in fact
it is a way of life
art imitates life

to a major degree
some imitators have no life
art has
   David Rosenthall

David Rosenthall is a writer and is based in Essex. His works
range from poetry to short stories. he also travels
extensively as a musician.

Confrontation - for Kate Adie

What happened to him I'll never know
His was just a face in the crowd
A hand carrying a rag, printed with the word 'Liberty'
and eyes with that haunted, hunted stare.
Eyes that seemed to look straight into mine
As he flashed across our screen
But I often wonder what happened to him
He was no older than one of my sons.
Did all go well, did he go on to win
What he'd gambled his liberty on?
Or, as he raised his hand in protest
Was he picked off by a sniper's gun.
I've often woke in the night
Wondering if he ended up being tortured in an underground
His was the voice of the voiceless
Was it silenced forever in Tienenman Square?
But whether he lived or whether he died,
His battle's already won.
For what has been said cannot be unsaid
And what has been done has been done.
I shall always wonder what happened to him
Although I may never know
But not any more is he just a face in a crowd
For, truly, he is everyone's son.
   M. Appleby

Marjorie Appleby was born and lives in York, She is a member of York Poetry Society and her work has appeared in several literary magazines and anthologies.

Troubled Waters?

Through the years I have grown
(More weight to the bone!)
Auburn hair now peppered with grey
And wrinkles round my eyes have grown

Gone now my beauty of which I was proud
(Snatched away by time!)
Gone now are my impulsive ways
The grape has turned to wine.

More content, placid and calm?
The storm may rage within
But tempered now with reasoning
Sees the folly of youth's days;
And now wisdom comes -
Like the wine from the grape,
Matured, full-bodied, no longer sweet -
And pours itself like oil upon the
Troubled waters...
So smooth, to hide the turbulence below!
    Lynn Sykes

Lynn Sykes was born in 1946, married and living in Milton Keynes, she works as a secretary for a charity that helps people with disabilities. Enjoys reading and writing poetry.

The Shrine

The shivering crowd
Patiently wait at the
Shrine of the mobile god.
Time passes slowly,

As if a weight
Were holding the
Clock's hands back.
One God rushes by,
Ignoring the wet throng.
'Full' they murmur to one another,
Congregation late again.
Once more the hands
Of the clock
Slowly tick away their lives,
Their god is sighted
'Bout time an' all'
Gods flock accepted
Another miracle to lead
Wayward home.
Gifts of gold
Are ceremoniously
Placed on the
Collection plate,
Near the disciple
Of the faith.
   Kip Porteous

Kip was born in Carrickfergus in 1964, lived in Scotland for
twelve years, now lives in Leeds. He works in printing and
has been scribing for eight years. His hobbies include
sculpture, travelling and hedonism.

The Sun

Melted
Into the sky
So bright
So light
Sunset.

Melted,
Red as the fire,
Fading,
Nothing,
Darkness.

In glory
The great light has come
Dawning
Brightly,
Morning.
    Charlotte Whitchurch (Aged 11)

Charlotte Whitchurch is eleven years of age and lives in
Shoreham by Sea. A pupil at Davison High School for Girls,
Worthing, she finds great enjoyment in writing.

Web of the Mind

It came from the tangled corners of a spider's web,
With hairy arms and short tubby legs,
Eyes on stalks and non hearing ears,
A large furry body and a noise that sears,
Brown and purple, black and red,
It travels so quietly like the living dead,
In the darkened recess behind the fridge,
Over the door used for a ridge,
In the night or day, dark or light
Lurking by the light switch just to give you a fright,
A weary head on a warm white pillow, sinks into sleep,
Is it an hour or a minute, an eye open for a peep,
You think it's there, or maybe not,
Perhaps it was a dream, or what, or what,

It's silent nothing stirs, but something purrs,
A rush of air surrounded by fur,
A chomping of jaws and a more contented purr,
Now it's gone, the thing,
This or that, but just a minute,
I haven't got a cat...!!!
    D. C. Buffrey

Douglas Buffrey is a 44 year old Scorpion who lives with his wife and children in Cheltenham. This is his first poem to be published which he dedicates to Candice with love.

Untitled

Rainbow apple of my eye
Strawberry and blackcurrant pie
What an incredible sight
A bonfire, flames alight
Sparrow, gull, blackbird, sky
Guy Fawkes night, time to die
Ashes to ashes, dust to dust
Swing the sparkler if you must
Keep your head, keep control
Watch the spirit, feel the soul
Old aged pensioner, little child
The old, the sad and the beguiled
Superman's coming, look above
A white ceiling, with a tiny dove
A time to live, and then you cry
in the tunnel; at the end you die
A phoenix arisen from a single flame
Nor you or me are here to blame
Now the teacher calls my name

And here I am, as before, the same
Teach' drones on that little bit more
I find my eyes steadfast on the door
And once again I'm bored once more
    D. W. Inness

David Inness was born in Durham and is currently a student in London. This is his first published poem though he hopes to have more work published in the future.

The Old Tin Bath

The old tin bath,
I remember so well,
Hanging on the back yard wall.
Every Friday night,
It was lifted down
Then each one, in turn
Shed all.
Soap and towel,
Clean nightwear,
Were ready as the bath was filled.
Jug by jug, all clean and fresh,
Not a drop of water was spilled
The first one in,
Had to make it brief,
Clean water was luxury enough!
The next one in,
Had the water cooled down,
And the next and the next had it rough.
For the last in the bath it was a downright shame,
As no-one could be more unlucky,
Than to sit in a bath,
With it's secrets held fast,
And the cold water now turned mucky!
  Gwyneth Cleworth

Gwyneth Cleworth was born and still lives in Bolton where she works in local government. Having had one poem published previously and several appearing in local press she wishes to continue writing poems and short stories.

P. S.

After the written
Will the words vanish, like passing ephemera
Into the black hole of night?
Or will they endure, neat in alphabetical tomes,
To reach through the centuries
And comfort the afflicted,
Or woo for a tongue-tied lover?

After the written
Will the words lie - lavish, scrolled -
Age-long in the cool vaults of the earth,
Each character, fresh-flourished from the caliigrapher's brush
Yet imbued with an ancient wisdom?

Or will they be carved, starkly, in stone,
Runic symbols to baffle, tantalise;
Waiting for time to polish away the meaning,
Leaving just the magic?

After the written
Did the first words,
Scratched, - shaky, hesitant - in the sand
Cause early man to shout with a new joy?
A joy undimmed, even by the washing waves;
For just to have written
Is a unique privilege.
   Marion Whistle

Marion Whistle works in north London as a computer
programmer/analyst. She has had several poems published
in anthologies; and also enjoys entertaining locally with 'The
Manor Singers'.

Atomic Winter

With intense pain and peeling skin
the mushroom cloud has reached within.
Organs scream and burst apart,
eyeballs melt, fear stops the heart.
Lonely winds whip skeletal trees
outstretched branches stripped of leaves beg; and freeze.
Dust and debris fights for place,
this war was to be our saving grace.
Instead no victor is in sight,
to shamble through this permanent night.
Silence takes over as the world grows cold,
frigid twists of metal embrace and fold.
Wrapping around charred flesh, ragged clothes.
Only the rats remain in droves.
    Delyse Harrison

Delyse Harrison is a mature student living in Bradford. She
writes short stories and poetry as a hobby.

If Only

If only you were a figment of my imagination,
Or a mere fragment of my memory.
If only my lips were numbed
So that I could not remember the touch of your kiss.
    Tatyana Zadyraka

Tatyana Zadyraka is currently in her final year at college
studying Russian Language and Soviet Studies. She is the
daughter of a Ukranian immigrant.

The Gulf

We watched today from your bedroom window
The blackbird's flit, to fence, to apple tree.
You didn't see what I might see below
For I am thirty-six, you have just turned three.

As you searched your world for explanations
And pressed your fingerprints upon the glass
My thoughts had flown far, to baffled nations
Who wake in fear of hunger, pain and gas.

Those huddled stares that nightly fill the screen
From Africa, Baghdad and Israel
Reflect a world that's cruel and obscene,
Each dawn a footstep further into hell.

When we watched today from your bedroom window
The alley cats were running wild and free.
You didn't see what I might see below
The breadcrumbs and the feathers, that refugee.
   Declan C. McCotter

Declan C. McCotter was born in Co. Derry, Ireland in 1954.
He now lives in Manchester where he teaches mathematics
at Xaverian College. He began writing in 1990.

Autumn

Autumn is a tranquil time,
Leaves rustling to the ground,
Making a glowing carpet,
Of russet, gold and brown.
Blackberries ripening in the hedgerows,
Swallows on the wing,
Making their way to distant countries,
Leaving the robin to rule as king.

Autumn is so mellow,
Overhead there hangs a haze,
Softening all the colours,
To blend with Autumn days.
    Kathleen Dodd

Kathleen Dodd lives in Littleborough, almost on the border
of Lancashire and Yorkshire. She has always had a love of
poetry and enjoys composing it.

The Soldier on the Somme

Listing in the wind, the corpse swayed with the rhythm of
                                uncontrollable force -
The hollow sockets where young eyes, once gazed to the sun,
had gone, only the bones and a remnant of khaki showed
to the world. That war, is either joy or filled with remorse.
Joy for the victor's, but at a cost of death -
My body was young too, but my mind was old -
This trench, my home - the mud a bed -
But this mud is red - bloody with the comrades of yesterday.
'Oh God!' I cried, as I gaze at the corpse -
The broken limbs, the torso's, this is the thin red line,
Death means nothing, I keep saying, but yet I want to run
away, only my duty as a soldier of the king - kept me here,
in this stinking, slimy trench.
A shout goes up! we creep from our holes, -
Sweat, my eyes are filled, as I trudge noiseless across no
                                man's land,
My hand's frozen to a weapon of death -
When I get back to my trench, I must sleep,
sleep in the mud -
A light flashes, the blackened sky, 'Oh God' I cry again,
We go in, -

I trudge on, my thoughts, to my Mother, funny how, my
Mother, should I think,
I stumble, I see the mud, turn to red,
Some-one is hurt, death again,
Then I realise, the red is my blood -
I fall, fall, Mother, I am asleep,
asleep in the mud.
    Deanna Ginns

Deanna Ginns lives in Boston, Lincolnshire and has had many
poems published in magazines and books. Writes poetry on
the first world war, and is a member of The Western Front
Association.

Lady of the Night

I knew she was a prostitute because
She told me so; she trusted me perforce -
For I am of an age she would call old;
She was beautiful, not brash or harsh or cold,
Fair hair, blue eyes, soft skin, too deathly pale;
And when I asked her why, she could not fail
To see the look of pity in my eyes.
'You would not understand or realise,'
She said, 'I could but choose between two evils,
Drudgery, degradation - they are devils
Worse than I face now. I have no brains
For ought but menial tasks, nor, for my pains,
Sufficient beauty for a life in art,
Or on the stage and yet my restless heart
Longs for the ecstasy beyond the rainbow,
The feel of silk, the dazzling diamond's glow;
Tell me, in your wisdom, tell me how
Could I know ought without what I do now -
By servitude or factory chains or dole? '
I have no home, nobody, not a soul -
And the love I find is sometimes almost real -
And yet no words could tell you how I feel.'
'I could give you a home, a chance to change'

'No!' she said 'Too late to rearrange
My life, but thanks for trying, listening -
I see the city lights all glistening -
And beyond, the moon and sun - and I shall meet
A man who understands - falls at my feet
Knows me for what I am - and then forgives
Knows the longing that within me lives;
The cry for beauty that, deep hidden, lies -
The spark that life for some always denies -
And we shall wed - for years for this I've schemed -
And give our bairns the life we only dreamed!
But had you found me when I was a child
I would prefer to have been undefiled.'
    Monica Joy Laneby

Monica Joy Laneby has had poetry and children's stories
printed since she left school. She is a housewife, and worked
on Spitfires at Castle Bromwich during the war.

Season's Feelings

Fresh, soft flowers.
A new beginning.

A light, clean breeze.
New thoughts blossoming.

Grand, green trees.
Strength amounting.

Warm, mellowing rays
A sense of being.

A cool, gentle wind.
Mentally calming.

Leaves, golden brown.
Emotionally stirring.

Cold, misty skies.
Slowly deceiving.

Bitter, sharp gales.
Turmoil surrounding.

White, settling snow.
Erasing the pain.

Harsh, cleansing rain.
Fresh, soft flowers,
Again.
   P. McKissack

Polly McKissack is a 22 year old living in London. She spends most of her time looking after her young daughter and enjoys writing poetry and prose in her spare time.

Untitled

Oh, why does it always happen to me?
From thousands in town, why choose my chimney?
I thought it was all a fairy tale, a myth
This Santa Claus can't really exist!

But one Christmas Eve - the air was quite nippy
And 'Crash!' in the hearth this ageing plump hippy!
All dressed in red with white fluffy trim
I gave him a glass of my Dad's best sloe gin.
'Ho Ho Ho! that was good, let me have just one more!'
Then another and soon he's asleep on the floor!
He snored so loudly the whole house was shaking
Then I noticed outside - Christmas Morning was breaking!
I looked at his sack full of games, dolls and toys
And thought of all the sad girls and boys.
I tried to wake Santa, he was out like a light
I got him in this mess so I must put it right.
I put on his clothes and picked up his sack,
Leapt on the sleigh, gave the whip a good crack.

Soon we were flying high over the town
Delivering gifts, until we came down
Back at my house now where Santa had woken
(And do you know that he was still laughin' and jokin'?!)
He thanked me so much then went on his way
And I slept throughout that Christmas Day!
   Lucy Dayton

Lucy Dayton was born in St. Albans in 1967. She writes
poems and short stories as a hobby. This is her first to be
published.

For What

Watch the water, feel the breeze
See the birds fly by, with ease
Nature gave us all of these
For what?

Flowers growing, trees in bloom
Summer will be coming soon
Wiping out all winters gloom
For what?

Dirty water, smoky air
Nature damaged beyond repair
All because we didn't care
So what?

It's not too late, things can be changed
If man would only re-arrange
Get back to nature, it's not so strange
Then what?

Polluted water, plants and trees
Life would return to all of these
Men would suffer less disease
For life!
   Alan Seymour

Alan Seymour is a draughtsman, living in s.e. London. He has written few poems but is encouraged by the good response they receive. His ambition is to have a book published.

Untitled

How much are we willing to sacrifice to satisfy our needs?
I'd give you my life,
And a lifetime of love,
But could I give you my dreams?
   Janine Kay

Janine Kay was born in Dorset in 1972. She is currently studying communication at a local college and intends to follow a career within the media.

Great Aunt Martha

On the corner,
My Great Aunt Martha standing there.
Beaded bonnet on her hair,
Dressed all in black;
Wished, that I could turn back,
But, I was on an errand,
And, could comprehend,
That she would wait for me,
And knew for certain,
What her words to me would be.

'Han't washed yer face yet then'.
My face was covered in freckles,
Was an embarrassment to me,
And her advice to me would be.
'Go to the meadow early,
And wash your face, in the dew,
On a cow pat'.
I never did that.

But now I am older,
And make-up in order,
I hide the freckles on my face;
And on my arms,
They take their place.
　　Evelyn J. Farmer

Evelyn Farmer lives in Somerset and is retired. She finds
pleasure in writing small poems with some success in local
magazines.

Child of Beauty

Child of beauty, come forth unto me
Bring me love in perfect harmony
Spread your wings and warm me with your sun
Enrich my soul and my spirit with you shall come
Bring into my life hope and happiness
'Tis you I love, this my soul doth confess
Shed light upon my mind and warmth in mine heart
As my body loves you, and I shall not part
Peace and harmony has come our way
Having enriched our lives in each new day
As yonder waves into the sea
My love, my life I give to thee
As yonder rolls the uncertainty of time
Dashing waves reach out as they decline
Fate and Destiny is in our hand
So let us, as the skies, to that peaceful land
　　Alison Cook

Alison Cook lives in the Yorkshire Dales, she has written
poetry and prose for many years and she hopes one day to
publish an anthology of verse.

2 A.M. Dreams

I'd just washed my hair
when somebody hammered on the front door.
I wasn't expecting any callers so I left it,
then out of the window I saw her next door
retreating furiously down the path,
that silly green anorak as always in attendance.
For some reason, hair dripping
I ran out into the rain and called her,
only to find myself
driving her and her idiot son to a restaurant.

They ordered mounds of food,
the smell lingered for an age in my nostrils
and was still evident on waking.
I wouldn't have minded all that
but for the life of me I couldn't think
why the hell I should give somebody I don't like
even in my wildest dreams,
a lift to the Chinese take-away.
   Jane Meadows

Jane Meadows lives in Coventry and runs a theatrical digs
for local theatres. She writes poetry and short stories in her
spare time.

Unknown Walker

Walks the streets without reason
eyes as angry as the storm
Punches your face with his stare

He say's people always talk about him
always a bad word too
he'll tell you
about his hardship
but question is would you care

Walk the streets without reason
people turn the other way
talks to himself in the window

It's not his reflection
it's a real person there.
   Rachel Davies

Rachel Davies was born in 1970. The owner of Psychedelic
Bazaar Alternative Stall at her local market where she lives
in Newport. Inspired by Glastonbury, The Doors and Seamus
Heaney.

Little Big Man

Small he was in stature, a little man,
he called himself a 'handy man'
No job he would not tackle, no task too
menial.
To give of his best, to him, came natural.
A caring, sharing, giving man,
an allayer of fears.
An arm-around-the-shoulder man,
a mopper up of tears.
A listening man, but free with advice,
generous with his laughter, truth in his
quiet eyes.
Like a ship that passes in the night,
he sailed away.
And life was never quite the same, from that
day.
I miss him very very much, his friendship and
his gentle touch.
Twas a pleasure to have met him, I'll not meet
his like again.
I shall never forget him, he was a giant
of a man.
   Kathleen Scully

Kathleen Scully is a housewife from London who has written poetry for her own enjoyment for many years. This is her first published piece.

Flowers

Golden rain, golden showers,
What lovely names we give to flowers
Ragged robins, lady's lace
The pansy with it's pretty face.

Larkspur pink, white and blue
Lady's slipper, lady's shoe.
Pimpernels and poppies too
Buttercups and cornflowers too.

Lavender and love in the mist,
Haste to the wedding and lover's kiss
Candytuft of every hue
Primroses, violets and heavenly blue.

Roses, cowslips and proud London pride
King cups and gold cellandine
Corncockle bright and chain of hearts
Lilies fit for a bride.

Sunflowers, moondaisies, Bethlehem star
Rosemary for remembrance, wherever you are.
Sweet William, sweet rocket, sweet peas climbing high,
Granny's nightcap and travellers joy.

Five fingers golden, clover and tare
Ladies mantle and gentlemen's hair.
Snow on the mountain, golden stone crop,
Creeping jenny, forget-me-nots.

Hairbells ringing in the rain
Daisies to make daisy chains
Oh, I could sit and think for hours
Of the lovely names we give to flowers.
   R. Anderton

Rose Anderton was born in Cheverton, Suffolk in 1909. She now lives in Frome, Somerset and spends her time knitting for Oxfam and writing poems, several of which have been published in church magazines and local papers.

Perception

Part of nature's sensory path,
Brilliance in every cavity of deep despair,
The line of truth and rediscovery
Of the birth of living
Each particle of time in
The rhythm of God's music.
A scent so painful, overwhelming
As it's power to heal, restore
More than beauty to serenity itself.
Senses abstract, transitory,
For each particle of time is
The rhythm of this state.
Grief lies immersed
In the torturous splendour
Of eternal bliss.
Word proclaim static emotions,
Sensations glisten and fold into
Each particle of time which is
The rhythm of eternity.
Subtly blending all sensation
Into the innermost desire to appreciate
God as a particle of time.
   Mary Vallender

Mary Vallender lives in Sutton Coldfield. She is a musician and teacher who writes poetry, songs, music and stories.

Sealed Fate

The cull was most decisive.
Man, the modern artist, had left his display.
Across the hard, white canvas of frost
Lay scattered pieces of grey,
Lumpy slumps of seal-pulps. litter
To the descending nemesis of sea-birds.

Careless brushstrokes of red marked trails
On the ice. Some scrawled uncertainly
To the edge, dripped into the cold sea-surface
And painted a shimmering path towards the sun,
Half-submerging its shame, tainted into silence.

You, who comfort us with guidance,
Culled from interstellar devices,
Apply for me now the means of your science
To these, born under the sign of Pisces.

The parent-hordes have left this snow,
Swimming in funereal procession;
Next year, they will want to know
The faults of their profession.

Astrologers! Dispense advice
Around this rudely-patterned ice;
Tell us, please, if what you see
Is man's concluding tragedy.
Once, we aspired to be wise,
Took our God for our disguise
And mated only in the fall.
Spring-born, we were Pisceans all.
  Hamlet

Hamlet is the pseudonym of a singer/songwriter resident in
Kent. Poetry credits include prize winning submissions
published in small poetry magazines. The writer is currently
engaged in producing a musical play concerning suffragettes.

Friendship

It is very rare in life you find a friend that's true
Someone you can really trust and cares for what you do
It helps to lift one's burdens and to give a little hope
So that whatever comes along somehow
You can cope with all the aggravations and frustrations that
                                                    you meet
It helps you see a little light in this worlds dark old street
So don't take that friend for granted that would be a
                                                    mistake
You will find that it's much better if you can give
                                              and not just take
   Margaret Esposito

Margaret Esposito was born and still lives in London. She
works full time as a general office clerk, when she retires
next year she would like to spend more time writing poetry.

The Lost Years

A babe, a boy, a youth, a man
Became a soldier, then began
His learning true,
Of starkness bare with hearing
Feeling and seeing too
The things that once were far away
Were now his neighbours night and day.

And dreams must come with mad intent
To shake the body which is spent
Then in the dawn he looks up
But only sees the shadows of destruction born
Of man's desire to wreck and spoil
The precious gifts from God to all.

Now the babe is old and grey,
No good has come from yesterday,
The sighs are long and often deep,
The head is bowed as if in sleep,
But the thoughts are clear
And the mind alive with questions still
Yet, although he knows the answer now,
He asks himself again,
Will world peace ever come?
No, no, it never shall.
  Fred Goodger

Fred Goodger is a retired factory shop-floor worker and war time Grenadier. Received little schooling but was educated by life itself. Commenced writing in 1985, poems and short stories, with his own style.

Rites of Passage

Those silver ribboned roads
Which wider were and where
We talked and argued through the night
To find a place to be
Have narrowed since.

Those seas which deeper were
And in whose singing tides
We twinkled starry rhymes
Of innocence and joy
Have jettisoned their quince.

And bridges where we walk
Are not the ones we had supposed.
Those forests in whose dappled shadows
Dwelled sublimer forms
Than I could show you now
Have buried secrets
Under dreams of stone.
Those cities whose bright streets

We mazed with rumour and with history
Have closed their gates
And all the tumult
Of their days is gone

And the twisting metaphor I framed
Is pinned against a whitewashed wall.
  Christopher Newton

Chris Newton was born in Southampton and teaches at a
primary school in Thanet. He has three children, and at 48
years old still plays football and cricket, competing at a
local level.

Motherhood

First two made one in marriage blessed by God
Then in due time a wondrous thing occurs
When consummation brings the fruit of love
And deep within one's being new life stirs.
Then microscopic cells will multiply, the tiny foetus grows
                                        until the dawn
Of motherhood when on the natal day fulfilment comes at
                                last - a child is born.
Now frequent cuddling and close caress
Will make the bonding that reduces fears
For it instils security and trust
That lead to confidence in later years.
In early days dependence is complete
Until beyond the home his world extends,

New skills are learnt and social contacts made
And gradually for himself he fends.
As childhood days go by, some discipline
Must go along with tender loving care
So when the young go out into the world
Their attitudes and judgements will be fair.
In teenage years some problems there will be
And these may well cause family stress and strain
But adolescence passes and in time the loving family ties
                                    prevail again.
The years go by, the child becomes a man
Or woman growing up in truth and grace
The strings are cut, and rightly so, for then
The adult in society has a place.
It seems as if one's task has now been done
But Motherhood's a never-ending state
And offspring who are loved and then released
Their years of care will now appreciate.
    Marcelle D. Williams

Marcelle Williams is a science graduate living in Wokingham.
She has written for local newspapers and supports many
charities, especially those concerning animals. She paints in
water-colour and is involved in church work.

Long View

Glass horizons shatter
Sky slides down
And mountains somersault
As earth's hand flings us all away
Back where we came from
Dust to dust
And into stars
That shine in other skies
Delighting
Strange new worlds
New kinds of people.
    Maurice Liddiard

Maurice Liddiard formerly taught English and drama in Essex and has published plays. He now lives in Sussex.

Sunshine

As the sands of time pass us by
We awaken
We stumble
The day darkens
We rise
We fall
A new beginning.
  Nicola-Jayne Davies

Nicola-Jayne Davies is 20 years of age, she has lived in Basildon, Essex all of her life and has been writing poetry and short stories for the past two years.

The Genius of Man - Seduced by Life

A giant; he rose and tore apart the rose shot clouds of
                                        morning.
Bright fire flared from his spurning heels -
Sheets of sparks from his fingertips spanned the fading stars.

Drenched in the red, rich wine of life's bright day
His feet stumbled, oh! so slightly,
In the dark brown foothills of the afternoon,
The fierce eagles gaze flickered once -
Swift as a bat's wing.

The purple haze from the dark hollows of the evening
Speared his flesh to the heart.
The golden muscles flagged and twisted.
With his first sigh he gently parted the shades of night,
Then passing, let them fall, rustling, on an empty stage.
  John Russell Bohun

John Bohun lives in rural Hampshire and has recently retired
to the enjoyment of birdwatching, reading and writing poetry.
He hopes one day to publish a 'slim volume'.

Spring '91

We sat to eat,
Our hot-cross buns,
Where multitudes,
Of daffodils,
On grassy banks,
Stood tall. At noon
Bright rays of light,
Shone through stain'd glass,
Crimson and blue,
And Christ was there.

After the sun
Became obscured,
The North-east wind,
Once more assailed
The city walls
Remorselessly.
And daffodils,
Bowed low in prayer,
For forebearance,
To Jesus Christ.

Tired of running,
Before the chill
Black clouds paused when
The wind drew breath.
Bright sunlight fled
From the stain'd glass.
And pilgrims who
Walked down below,
Forgot Kurdistan,
And lost sight of Christ.
        L. Wickham

Leslie Wickham, poet, writer, born in Tickhill, writes to expand his literary interests and hopes to publish more of his work.

Last Word

'When I was a lad,'
Says my Grandad,
'I didn't cry for the moon.
I had to get up early
And milk the cows,
And feed the pigs,
And groom the horses,
And draw the water,
And collect the eggs,
And scare the rooks,
And polish the boots,
And sweep the yard,
And flea the dog.
All for sixpence a week.
You don't know you're born!'
Says my Grandad.
'But, you never would wash
Behind your ears!'
Says my Grandma.
   Lucy Crisp

Lucy Crisp was born in Suffolk, she has a lifelong interest in writing poetry and short stories and painting with pastels and watercolours.

Naturally

With smiling and contented face
I gaze in perfect wonder at my nation's beauty.
Far from the bustle of life's daily race
Removed from any sense of duty.

I scarcely know which way to turn,
Such is the divinity of all before me.
In this cherished and wondrous place,
There is nothing that the eye does not wish to see.

Forests of trees stretch out for miles,
Dotted on a flowing carpet of green.
Wildlife freely and unhindered roams
Throughout this picture-postcard scene.
And accompanied by a lulling breeze
Birds sing in choruses of musical bliss.
Unspoilt by the blight of human noise,
Picture no paradise greater than this.

I spare a short, yet worrying thought
For the world that exists beyond my recess.
Where greed and progress are significant words
And money is the measure of all success.
It seems that man has no need for nature,
Whilst comfort and technology dominate his plan.
But if mankind could survive without this,
Just think how the earth would thrive without man.
    Stuart Wickham

Stuart Wickham was born in Bath in 1968. He is pursuing
a career in banking and hopes to have his poetry and other
work published at some time in the future.

A Country Dance

Come, let's away, and to the dance;
Those merry eyes and upward glance
And lovely rhythm of their limbs
Shall lure us too, and set our whims
To that gayer music, lighter measure
So crowned with sun and linked in pleasure.
We'll gather to the pipes sweet air.

So face to face with laughter there
And sunlight bright on cheek and brow
We all shall take our choice, and now
Moving in grace, we, thee shall pass
Lithe-footed down the shadowed grass;
From breathless beat to softer change
All through the music's lilting range.

While breezes stir amid the green
So drawn into the deepening light
Close touched with magic, sound, and sight
Of maids and men, unburdened, free,
We'll drift in dreamlike ecstasy.
'Till dusk, blue-veiled, has filled the land.
And drowsy partners, hand in hand.
Shall stray to meet the harvest moon.

Now lingering for a spell till soon,
With laughter stilled and dancers gone
We near to sleep and now alone.
We'll leave this quiet deserted vale
To silence and the nightingale.
    Margaret Brunwin

Margaret Brunwin is a widow who now lives in Somerset.
She has always had an interest in poetry, and lately, writing
verse for pleasure. None of her poems, till now, have been
submitted for publication.

Stumbling, Drunken

An old man came stumbling drunken through the night
Mumbling sad dreams that have revealed to him a sad plight
Remembering the love in a now lonely night.

'Listen to me! Listen to me!
With her I've danced in the warmth of a wild winter wind
Only to be blown away by her beautiful breath
Now she's gone, beauty is bleak

So I'll dance with death
The orchestrated sound of lamentful waves
Echoed sadness in my mind's caves.
She ran like a nymph of night on the beach
past a foaming sea,
She ran out of reach
Her ways tormented by beckoning me.
She laughed that in hours time
shyfully would come the illuminating
light of a frightened sun.
And abandoned I would fly like a
raging hawk, listening to the deranged
whisper of her deceitful talk.

And now stumbling drunken through the night
I come,
Remembering the loneliness I felt with the
frightened sun.
   Edward Donnelly

Edward Donnelly was born in 1971, originally from
Newbridge, Co. Kildare. Recently studying in Bolton Institute
of Higher Education, Lancs. When his course is finished he
hopes to get involved in writing.

Looking to You

Nature's jewel
Hanging, waiting, looking to you -
Tempting you.

It tempted others,
This undeniably beautiful gem,
Looking to you -
Perfection at it's best
And yet so simple in it's form.

As yet unmarked, untouched
But looking blatantly permissive and adult.
And looking to you
Through it's cloak of green foliage
Enticing, winking, flirting
When the gentle breezes
Push it to and fro,
The nature's jewel.
   Rasa E. Petris

Rasa E. Petris was born in 1946, is Lithuanian and has lived
in England for 40 years. At present studying social
Psychology and literature. Writing is her first love; one
ambition is to write a novel.

The Mystery that is Man

To get inside the heart of a man
Is akin to opening a can
Without a key of any kind
Perhaps the solution is in the mind

One day he's soft and close to tears
Tender, caring, oh so dear
Then when you think you know him well
Back he'll hasten to his shell

His work he carries everywhere
Wives, relations, friends, all share
His ups, his downs, his triumphs too
Although it's all just a bore to you

In sport he always must excel
Be tough and self-assured, or else
He'll take off to a quiet spot
With hook and line or perhaps a book

Some are of the pompous kind
We must all admire his mind
Eager to expound his views
First with all the latest news

It is so hard to find the heart
The point at which we can start
To really get to know him well
And let us enter to his shell.
   Clarice Oddy

Clarice Oddy was born and still resides in Gainsborough,
Lincolnshire. She is at present compiling a collection of her
work.

Rendezvous

From the moment we are born, our name goes in a book,
No mind can see it written no eyes can take a look.
The writing is invisible, the pen that writes it too,
Filed away by unseen hands, until it's time to view.
By us it's then forgotten, this never ending list.
Now can we remember? 'til we learn it must exist.
A library full of unread words, stacked high on unseen
                            shelves,
No conscious recollection, we placed them there ourselves.

There are tales of heroes and brave deeds yet untold,
Side by side with stories, we hope will not unfold
Millions of epics, no ending and no start,
And yet a kind of feeling you know it in your heart.
They say there's seven chapters called ages of each man,
But which is right in time or place, to link up with each
                            plan.
It's all an unsolved puzzle, an answer hard to find,
Treading on the unlit path, of your subconcious mind.

You'll have to travel by-ways, of lengths you do not know,
Or stand there at the cross roads, what does the arrow
                                                    show?
A rainbow waiting for you, has it been there all the time?
Hiding just behind the hill, you found so hard to climb.
Seven wonders of the world, you hope to find them all,
There's also Spring and Summer, to follow Autumn's fall.
Happiness surrounds you, it's finger lifts to beckon,
Precious moments tick away, that time just has to reckon.

You live in hope, the years roll on, you hope you've played
                                                the game,
Remembering the golden book in which they placed your
                                                    name.
The pages slowly turning, it's been so through the age,
A misted hazy finger, to point your special page.
A lifetimes questions answered, all will be revealed,
The timeless countless secrets, so openly concealed.
A sense of peace, a smiling face, a gently kind of nod.
You can keep that special Rendezvous, that Rendezvous with
                                                    God.

   Vera Oxley

Vera Oxley has written her own autobiography, a novel and
many poems, which have appeared in anthologies in London
and America. Vera is Manchester born but now lives in
beautiful Scotland.

The Hunt

'Tis a hunting, we will go today, dressed in garments bright
                                                and gay,
To get ready for the poor, unsuspecting, innocent victim of
                                                the day.
Folk all look fine, robed in garments, rich with colours of
                                        bright red and gold,
Villagers come out to praise and pray? Perhaps? And curse,
                                who knows, both young and old?

Sun is shining, the day is just right for the 'kill'. All is well
as off they set,
To chase forth into hill and dale and glen and soft woodland
glade, dew soft wet.
Loud thud of hoofs, all eager to claim, in their 'kill' of the
day, with dogs run amok,
Thundering along, with ears to the wind, and scent in the
air, of it's victim, hidden in crag and rock.

The poor frightened animal, all alone and so very afraid,
Terrified, in this, to him, his enchanted, lonely, sun-lit glade.
What have I done? He so piteously, in fear and anguish doth
cry?
Why must I be cornered? See, I have no chance but to lay
down and die.

I too, am one of God's children and one day we will meet,
face to face,
Will I see tears of remorse, will I perhaps, find just a trace
Of pity? Will you say to God that your friend, who fired
the bullet and aimed only to kill?
Scored only too well, as he showed off his 'wonderful' skill?

Did you see the blood, that spurted from my wounded side?
Were you there among the 'magic' and sadness of those who
cried?
Or, did it make you human enough, to feel sick and faint
and very ill?
Did you, watch this, God's creature, die and linger and lie,
silent and so still?

Did it satisfy you, your cruel need for an angry, spiteful
gun?
To shoot and blood the green fields, to stain, just for laughs
and such fun?
I guess you did laugh at your 'conquests', as you drank your
well-earned beer?
But those in Heaven. (On the 'other side'), put another mark
against you, not to cheer.

Just suppose that you were that defenceless animal or frail
                                        bird of prey?
Lying there lonely, wounded at the end of the day?
Too weak perhaps to cry, to weak to even get a drink,
Pause, 'ere you pull that trigger. Just pause and then think.
    Eve May Onslow

Seven A.M. in the Smoke

'No Surrender'
The motorists' battle-cry
Echoing through the smog and fumes
Furiously-pedalling cyclists,
Sinisterly masked,
Towing technology in their slipstreams.
Legions of static transporters
Slowly going nowhere.
Human perambulaters
Reeling them in one by one.
Phantom headlines flashing before my eyes
Four Pedestrians Maimed,
But He Gained Two Car-Lengths.
Onwards to the asylum!
    T. O'Brien

Tom O'Brien is London based and has been writing for two
years. He has had several articles and short stories published
and is looking for a publisher for his novel. This is his first
attempt at poetry.

Personal Poetry

I write my personal poetry
But never read what I've done,
'Cos that'd be bloody stupid.
Who said poetry had to be fun?

I scribble here and scribble there
I jot across the page.
And when this weary labour's done
I rip it up in rage.

I don't know what the trouble is,
Perhaps I don't take time.
But every time I write it out,
It never seems to rhyme.

Now this may sound quite silly
But it makes me quite irate,
So I'm going to become a Quantity Surveyor.
    David Newell

David Newell is based in North Wales, this is his first
published work, but with luck, will not be his last.

Feeling Nothing

I cannot define the difference
Between reality and fantasy
Drifting in and out of consciousness
Sleep, dream, sleep, awake
I am numb, no feeling
Comes from within, cold as ice
Sentimental fool I am
Clinging to every word
Listening for every heartbeat
I feel nothing, nothing.

No sound comes from my lips
Corners of my mouth turn down,
Robotic movements I make
No memory of previous days,
Time is passing, no calls
I just sit and wait,

Round and round in circles
Is how we live our lives
How I long for the rain
To wash away the pain.

Love changed my life completely
Lost love is hard to take
I hear the sound of raindrops
Still I feel nothing, nothing.
   Keely Nethercott

Keely Nethercott was born in London in 1969. She writes
poetry, short stories and articles. She has also written a first
novel, and currently works as a P.A.

The Seer

So ends the dark night of my troubled soul,
As in the clear dawn's resurrecting light,
I glimpse a radiant vision of the true whole
Vast full measure of eternity.....A sight
So glorious to behold, where rich and poor,
(The faithful and the true with loving heart)
Were standing there to greet me at the door,
Bright figures clad in light, who drew apart
The veil that hid me from the ones I love;
So shall I ne'er fear death's enduring will,
But lift mine eyes up to the one above,
Whose all protecting arms enfold me still,
The Christ who died and rose again for me,
That in eternity, I shall be free!
   Bryan Newey

Bryan Newey was born in Keighley, West Yorkshire in 1926,
but spent his lifetime in London. In his spare time he loved
writing poetry, hymns and contributing articles for church
magazines. Tragically he died following his retirement in
1991.

Too Late!

Like a butterfly born
On the last day of summer
Emerging at dawn
Awakening from slumber

The sun too weak to bring
Warmth to your wings
New life sounds around you
As distant bells ring.

Your beauty unseen,
No dancing in flight
Just a few hours
In summer's last light.

Dew drops around you
It's cool in the shade
Now silence surrounds you
As the summer light fades.

The last, all alone
The butterfly waits
Searching the sky
For a welcoming mate.
Alas for the butterfly,
Born too late.
    Mark Newman

Mark Newman was born in 1962 and currently lives near
Hampton Court. He writes for children and adults and hopes
to publish a first collection shortly.

Guilt

Agony of minatory,
Is penance of the innocent.
Sorrow of the happening,
Incites no repent.
Seasons of emotion,
Are memories of shame.
No thought to future,
Existence with blame.
Punishment of violation,
Judgement a pretence,
Sentence superficial,
Judicially no sense.
    Sharon Moore

Sharon Moore was born and still lives in Selby, she started writing poetry while still at school and has written for her own pleasure until now.

Red Nirvana

Through the dark descent of a thousand dreams
Locked in silence and as one;
An image breaks of cracking glass,
It's jagged shards now bearing down
Upon the floor of painted hearts,
Fragment and crumble on the ground,
And trodden in with unseen feet,
Hidden well - may soon be found.

And through this scene a barefoot child,
Feet glazed in red, gently steps.
Within the space of other minds,
Locked down deep in other heads.
They shake whilst sleeping, deadened arms,
Twitching muscles in their legs.
A thousand dreams a thousand screams,
A thousand lifeless on their beds.

Through the blaze of night, a million worlds,
Locked together around one sun.
An image shows of yielded faith
With its poisoned claws now bearing down
Upon the floor of eternal hope,
A hope that crumbles on the ground.
It is trodden with unseen hate,
Hidden well and never found.
    Anthony Mayle

Tony Mayle was born in 1968 and has lived in London all
of his life. He writes a great deal of poetry and lyrics and
is currently working on a novel which should be completed
by next year.

Suicide

Death does seek me out this night,
through this dark abyss that is my mind.
Silent cries that were never heard,
are lost forever in this psychotic world.

No time to think, nowhere to go,
must life be this forever more.
Artistic expression is what I seek
to bare my soul, to be free.

No reason I see to carry on
my will to live is dead and gone.
And so my friends, the time is near,
No more sorrow, no more tears.

Joyous freedom is mine at last,
pain and suffering have long since past
forgive me now, what I have done
blame not yourself, blame no one.
    Shaun McGrath

Shaun McGrath was born in Oldham in 1970. His interests include writing poetry and articles on various subjects.

The Patron Saint of Big Hearts

Just listen to her eyes
She's screaming to be free
Not a patch on her previous self
How you loved the light from her face
Of course, it's different these days
She's been captured by her own body

The Kamikaze man just kept plodding on
She still meant the same to him
Even when she shouted, he was calm
'here' he said 'cling to my arm'
If only she'd laugh like before
often she cried, but who would wipe his eyes

She gets frustrated, she's got her pride
Stop her world, end the ride
This has gone on for too long
There's a moral dilemma here
Only one man supported her from the start
Thank goodness for the Patron Saint of Big Hearts

Answer me this question please
Why does Mother Nature allow this
Does God feel ill at ease?
Is it better we don't understand
The Patron Saint looks pale and thin
Is anyone going to care for Him?
   Paul Maslin

Paul Maslin was born and still lives in the Wiltshire countryside, He originally started writing with the idea of his work being used as lyrics for songs but has recently switched to poetry.

A Tender Frenzy
(Tribute to Vincent Van Gogh.)

In sombre tones, impasto, brown,
Bowed shadows plough a sun scorched ground;

Above the corn a lark soars free
Tracing instincts infinity;
Flowering stars shedding glory,
Transform a gay Parisian story;

A rush of brushwork, deep impassioned eyes,
Rich orchards flourish through translucent skies;
Startled by joy upwelling pigments sing,
Restoring shaping gathering in the spring;
Landscapes escape - a radiance spills -
Indwelling springtime weathers hills;
Bright crests of paint - bedazzled braid,
Arise baptise form light and shade;
A Tender frenzy, wild, sublime,
The soul distills earth's paradigms;

The swirling cypresses arise,
Like premonitions in disguise;
Suns spin skies tremble whirling clouds
Breed apparitions wreathed in shrouds;
Skeletal trees contort twist strain,
Bent crippled limbs enacting pain;
A cornfields yields cacophonous crows,
Hell's bats, disturbed, the anguish grows.
Dave Mason

Dave Mason was born in Blackpool. He is currently working on more poems, contemporary song lyrics and his first novel.

Relinquished Memory

Do I know this place?
Have I been here before?
Is that my street exposed
- with rows of houses
half dismantled
laid to waste, silent, desolate
beheaded, eyeless, entrance free
standing like relics
of the ancient past
without name, without date
unqualified as a tourist trap
- except for me?

But then I am not sure.
Disclosed the flower paper
pasted with loving care
now faded and torn
by rough unfeeling hands.
But did not those workmen know
with tiles displaced
they released secrets of long ago
- laughter, joy and tears?

Do I know this place?
I do not think I do.
I turn and walk the other way.
   R. J. Marston

Joseph Marston was born in Leicestershire in 1921. Now
retired, he attends a creative writing class. Success came
in 1989 with his first published poem.

Sunday

Dreary day, Sunday.
Melancholy greys this autumn day.
Sombre sounds from birds in trees
Or overhead in the lazy breeze.
They cross the 'cut' to circle round
Solemn girders rising
From the dampening and leaf matted ground.
They take the form of cranes and jibs,
Of rusting metal tumbled down
Besides the weary, creaking bridge.
      Andrew J. LeMaitre

Andrew LeMaitre is 46 years old, was born in Middlesex but
has lived in Northamptonshire for the last 16 years. He has
been writing poetry since his schooldays.

The Oozle and the Oobly

The Oozle was known to be
something he couldn't,
we knew that he wouldn't
though between you and me
they all said he shouldn't.

The Oobly was always strange
his mind had come adrift,
he said he had a gift
I think his brain was rearranged
he'd look at you as if -

Try hard as I, they would not
even though they said
At least that's what I read,
they wished that I would get the knot
or possibly drop dead.

Then I realised that I
was getting past myself,
like talking to an elf,
how and which and where and why.
White rabbits on the twelfth.
    Geoffrey Lock

Geoffrey Lock is a bookbinder who lives in Great Yarmouth.
He has had Letter of the Week published in Punch Magazine
and his interests include genealogy.

Old Daniel

His duties were not written down;
talk about wages caused the vicar pain;
the subject never got discussed,
and so they stayed the same.

He loved the place, the sexton's cottage
by the old black yew looked out on
generations of his kind, their names
less legible each time he looked.

At weddings he would smile encouragement
at nervous brides; at funerals console
with simple words; and grieving widows
gratefully passed on their husband's clothes
to Daniel's careful wife who'd put in tucks
and let down trouser legs.

His days revolved around the church.
No bible-thumper, he had known the hell
of France, had lost his faith along with
comrades killed. But still some old
emotion stirred at evensong when choir and
organ touched some buried chord.

His own last service came in time;
the villagers turned out in force.
The curate supervised old Daniel's end
seeing it was the vicar's morning off.
   Phil Powley

Phil Powley is a retired lecturer, living in Lymington. His
short stories and poems are strongly influenced by boyhood
memories in the Weald of Kent.

Snowflakes

Softly falling,
Sky thick with icy feathers,
Flakes of contemplation.

As each lands, it is no
Longer a flurry,
or a skirmish - as of thoughts;
but a single unique entity.

Able to be distinguished, given
Space, before it warms, melts,
Is gone forever.

Only the memory remains.
   B. Sear

Brenda Sear was born in London but has lived in Cowes, Isle
of Wight for the past 18 years. She began writing poetry
18 months ago.

Down to the Sea

Rivulet, rivulet where are you going?
Down to the river, down to the sea.
Beautiful rivulet why are you rushing?
I want to grow bigger, I want to be free.

Cool, lucent stream why do you hurry
O'er boulders and gravel, past spinney and lea?
Do you know your meandering, clear crystal waters
Give pleasure to myriads of people like me?
Dirty great river, so yellow and muddy
Carrying pollution, dead fish and the trunk of a tree,
No longer lovely, your burden deposit
In harbour, splashing it up on the sides of the quay.
Rivulet, rivulet are you quite happy
Now that you've got there, now that you're free,
Did you sigh for the mountains when you came to realise
A mere drop in the ocean is all that you'll be?
    Audrey E. Simmons

Audrey E. Simmons is a retired home economics teacher.
She is the co-ordinator of a senior citizens group, who likes
classical music and knits small jumpers for refugees via
Oxfam.

Untitled

Two men sat on a bench
Talking as ever about a wench
Who was passing.
Her legs were oak, massing
Upwards to gargantuan cheeks
And monstrous girdle. Two weeks
Stubble on her chin -
There was no discussion of sin
From the two sages.
They smiled and bet their wages
That she was a metric tonne.
Give her another cream laden bun.
    A. C. Taylor

Anthony Taylor is a full time Lancastrian living in the South
East. Some of his verse has been published in magazines but
is mainly scurrilous or private.

The Piper

A picture in my mind
And warmth that's from behind
A face of stars and sunshine

The future isn't clear
A love I hold so dear
And yet I can't reveal it

Piper, you play your song so well, a tune that haunts me,
And weaves a magic spell which fills my heart.
How good it feels!

Piper, I'm dancing to the song that comes from within you,
And how can this be wrong - the way I feel
You play so well!

An aching in my heart
Each time that we're apart
I long to hear you playing.

The music that you sound
Echos all around
Can music last forever?

Piper, you always sound so good, I've had to follow
In any way I could - is it enough to keep in tune?
Piper, oblivious to the course and all around me,
From melody's true source - A happy cadence?
We've come so far!
   Jules Anthony

Jules Anthony hails from the Welsh Valleys and enjoys
writing from the heart - not from the head. Hopefully, the
new found inspiration for recent work produced will last
forever.

Frog

I sat eating my breakfast the other day,
Reading the paper whilst munching away,
All of a sudden I heard a loud scream,
It was my mum and she looked slightly green,
My breakfast flew one way, the paper went the other,
I looked up and said 'What's wrong Mother?'
Mum looked at the floor, I followed her eyes,
And what I saw took me by surprise,
For there sat a frog as still as can be,
I looked at mum and she looked at me,
She asked 'How on earth did that get in here?'
I replied 'I really have no idea',
I said, 'Maybe it want's to read the sports page,
But I'm reading this paper so it'll just have to wait'
We captured the frog with a fishing net,
I offered the sports section but it replied 'I've read it'.
   Louise taylor

Louise Taylor is twenty years of age and a qualified
hairdresser from Stevenage. She enjoys writing poems and
her ambition is to have her own collection published.

Adam

Adam is here, asleep and still,
Soft, round, pink and beautiful
Wrapped in a blanket in his proud father's arms,
I see you for the first time my son.

A shock of dark hair, a little button nose,
Chubby cheeks and a little double chin,
Weighing in at birth at 8lb 11oz.,
I see you for the first time my son.

Here is a child born of the miracle of life
From a seed of the Mother of Creation,
A baby, a person, flesh and blood,
And I see you for the first time my son, and love you.
    S. J. Taylor

S. J. Taylor was born in Vancouver, Canada in 1955 but has
spent most of her life in Derbyshire where she enjoys writing
poetry and doing craft work.

Untitled

Mary Judith Zatapan,
Dearly loved by this poor man,
But from a distance quite discreet
Must his one sweet avowal make,
Simply for conventions sake...
Convention binds us to our fate
But each soul has a true soul-mate
And she was his as time will tell
The future will all doubts dispel.
A sidelong glance, a secret smile,
This was his love a little while,
No more was given, or yet received,
But love expressed was thus relieved.
Eternity's not long to wait
For such a love to consummate,
And maybe on some other plane
They may both live to love again.
    Norman Tidball

Norman Tidball has been a wartime sailor, a schoolmaster
specializing in music, English and drama, an
organist/choirmaster and a jazz musician. He also writes
songs for children.

So What, He's Dead

The pale face, peaceful in cosmetics:
Eyes, lips closed, no breath,
Purposeful in death,
His tie central, tight
Just as in life.

Grim, cold, unfeeling
Eyes, through steel-rimmed glasses,
Ice.

Do this
Boy
Boy do that
Stand up boy
No.

Tears the response he sought,
Love the rejection he wanted.

My father - so what?

He's dead.
    Peter Williams

Peter Williams lives in Tavistock, Devon, where, apart from teaching and writing, he watches theatre and rugby, plays squash and walks Dartmoor and the Rame Peninsula. He is looking for a publisher!

The Pride of Anglais

Oh! Bring back the Empire,
That mountain of triumphant desire,
The old age of ruling, towering above,
Oh! For the pride and power, rule Britannia's love.

Unite, unite for the Pride of Anglais,
Blessed Anglais, the burning bright candlais,
Flying the flag, red, white and blue,
Where the patriotic arc is clearly in view.

The capital class, all other nations bow down,
Come to us struggling country, we shall taketh you under
                                                own gown.
Oh! For the pride of Anglais, biting off more than is due,
Too much of a sway in favour of the privileged few.

Where is the Pride of Anglais?
Tearing apart on the inside,
Who shall fly the kite for Anglais?
After far too many strikes upon the backside.

Oh! For the Empire out-classed,
Firmly dissolved in all that has passed,
Come now, pull together for the Pride of Anglais
Or see it swallowed up amidst Europe's sinking
Sandglais.
    Kevin Watson

Kevin Watson lives in Dronfield near Sheffield. He has been
writing as a pastime for several years and hopes to have
more work published in the future.

Dreaming on the Tube

I wish I could go to work in style,
Not on the Tube each rock and roll mile.
Trying to get the last empty seat,
But often defeated, they tread on my feet!

I wish I could travel just like a toff.
A Roller's chauffeur his cap he would doff,
As he opened the door and helped me step down,
Outside my office, in old London Town.

Oh my I've been dreaming, here's Notting Hill Gate.
What a fight to get off, I know I'll be late.
With a whoosh and a roar that train doors do slam
Then up the escalator, what a great jam.

Panting and pushed, in a bit of a state,
Another bleak platform on which to wait,
A Circle or District to High Street Ken,
Repeated tomorrow, all over again.
John W. Warricker

John Warricker is resident in Bexley Heath, North Kent.
Has at one time or another been a Telecom engineer and
a court clerk. Now writes straight articles, fiction and
poetry.

The Sea Monster

Green is the sea by day, and black by night,
Dark is the cavern where the monster lies
Motionless, as he opens weary eyes
That pierce the gloom with ever failing sight.
He waits, as he has waited endlessly;
He dreams (and every dream is happiness)
Of shoreless seas, and water limitless,
When earth and sky were in their infancy.
When rain for forty days and forty nights
Swept down in torrents from a laden sky,
Submerged and drowned with dire ferocity
The tail-less, finless, scaleless parasites
Who walked with scorn upon the pebbled beach,
And flung their nets with murderous intent.
The man-destroying deluge, heaven-sent,
Brought peaceful power within the monster's search
Until, with disbelief and mighty roar
He watched the waters ebb, the sea subside,
The jagged peaks appear, the mountainside,
The grassy slopes and last, the pebbly shore.

The monster, tired and barnacled, has lain
For countless ages in the greenery gloom
Within the cavern, soon to be his tomb,
His wordless wish for rain and rain and rain
To fall and fall and flood the earth again.
  Irene Wilson

Irene Wilson lives in Frome, her hobbies are solving
crosswords puzzles, playing Canaster and Chess and
occasionally writing poetry.

Kent Cottages

Three cottages in a row
When built, I would not know
Weather boarding a little worn
Adds to the charm of these homes.

Painted white, as a tradition
Aide the wood from going rotten.
Windows, rather small but neat
No depth for a window seat,

Front doors of the old pattern
With latches on to fasten
Gardens full of lovely blooms,
Some are scented in the gloom.

Maybe standing here so long
Passing from father to son
Seasons have come and gone
Still they are someone's home.

We look upon these homes of Kent
With the white boarding at the front
We stop and think and wonder why
As we travel the by way

These cottages of old design,
With boarding in straight line
They are homes of character
And seen as no other.
  Una Woodward

Una Woodward was born in 1916 in Wales. A retired district
nurse, she started writing poetry 12 weeks ago. Volunteer
worker for Age Concern.

The Rise and Fall of a Snowman

The snow fell silently all through the night
much to the little girl's delight.
She dressed herself and out she ran,
trying to make herself a snowman.
The snowball grew larger but started breaking.
Pretty soon small arms and legs were aching.
Into the garden came Daddy and Mummy;
pom pom hat and big boots, they did look funny.
Please build me a snowman and build it up high,
and put a hat on it touching the sky.
Daddy makes a snowball firm and round,
rolls it through the snow with a crunching sound.
The snowball got larger and grew and grew.
'Hey, give me a hand, I'm doing this for you'.
At last it was built and was quite a sight,
top hat and cane and suit of white.
She danced round the snowman, he was her best friend,
and hoped their friendship would never end.
It's getting late and time for little girls to go to sleep,
She said goodnight to the snowman and had a little weep.
The night was warm and the snowman melted away,
he would not be there to see another day.
As he melted he seemed so sad,
his little friend won't see him again, too bad.
  T. M. Welling

Terry Welling, brought up in North London, joined the
Merchant Navy, moved to Coventry and now lives in
Leicestershire with his wife and daughter. Owns his own
greengrocer's shop.

Folly of War

Is mankind mad that he permits
This shedding of human wine?
Does he forget this life of ours
Was the gift of the Lord Divine?
And yet,throughout this world today
We see no love. instead
By man's own hand the virgin soil
Is spoilt by wasted dead.

This earth should be a happy place,
Where men can work and play,
But no! through jealousy and greed
We all turn out and slay.
Perhaps one day we'll see our wrongs
But dearly has it cost
We'll turn to God and follow Him
And find what we have lost.
    L. J. Watkins

Leslie Watkins was born in 1923. He served in the Royal
Air Force from 1941-46, Birmingham/West Midlands Police
Force from 1947-79. Assistant manager at City Law Courts
for 8 years and has now retired.

My Body

My body keeps new laws of it's own
Now it is no longer young.
Makes new shapes as it falls through the years
Ignores my sighs
My ageing tears

My Body makes new rules as it goes
Now on it's way
Down the hill
On it's nose.
I cannot watch
too sad to see
This unco-operative weary stranger
That once was...me.
   Kay Wolfsohn

Kay Wolfsohn is a Colchester housewife and mother who
prefers writing to housework and (husband please note) would
like a word processor, huge desk and comfy chair - for her
birthday.

Ode to Exercise

If you are losing weight you see
You really must be wise
So with your plan you must combine
Some regular exercise.

This need not be too drastic
And never hurt a lot
'Cos the body's not elastic
A yo yo you are not.

You could walk or jog or tap dance
Do yoga, swim or weight train
But what'ere you choose
You'll soon find out
Too much too soon will strain.

So take it slow, build up your pace
Get supervised perhaps
Or else you could end up with
Bad heart, sore limbs, teeth capped.

It's all in how you approach it
Be consistent, take some action
A little each day is better for you
Than ending up in traction.
  Geraldine White

Geraldine White is a frustrated tap dancer who is actually
a secretary in the City. She lives in Staines and hopes to
have more poems and short stories published in the future.

Mother Earths Corruption

Dark compulsive changes,
Imploding on our lives,
Traces of past agony,
Exploding terror cries,

Beneath the crumbling earth,
The throats of hell live on,
Evils passion for the death,
The life outside now gone,

Wandering through new ages,
Black ash from previous dead,
No signs of any living
To death the world was lead,

Predecease the darkest onslaught,
Impoverish damage unexplained,
Charred flesh, posing gore,
Uninhibited minds to blame,

Consumed by devious thoughts,
Predators of consumption,
Endless deaths, now no laws,
Dear mother earths corruption.
  Oliver Wilcox

Oliver Marc Wilcox was born in Ipswich in 1974. He writes short horror stories and is now working full time on his first novel, he hopes to become a full time professional.

The Death Bed

I slept but for a moment,
Foolishly, I'd dropped my guard
And waking, in an instant found myself cut off.
Encompassed by Death's courtiers,
My bed besieged by those who loved me most,
Unwitting servants of unwelcome host.

In vain, to arms my mind and spirit rose,
The body never moved, but broke the ranks
And cowered in the deep of tight tucked sheets.
Only the eyes responded to the reveille's call
Bright watchmen of the mind awoke, revealing all;
And finding no response within their rebel camp
Broke forth with silent weeping at the cause.

Then daylight dipped as morning mellowed on
The countenance of loved ones fell in sympathetic vein
And warm upon my face I felt the sunbeams rain
Darkly, as the town clock claimed the noon-tide hour
And peering from within, those silent sentinels
Ceased their weeping;
And through narrowing horizons grasped at those they loved
Who all at once, ceased their dulcet murmurings
And statue still, stood fixed upon a painted room-scape,
And all the world was dead, still standing on its feet.
   Nicholas Whitchurch

Nicholas Whitchurch runs an accountancy practice in Shoreham, Sussex. He has also written script and song lyrics (Music by Rachel Wilton) successfully performed locally. His heart was always in poetry, but he is only now considering publication.

Poetry

Heroes compose prose
Adverse to converse in verse
To mime a rhyme
To chime in time
Poetic justice

It's erudite to recite
Creation without specification
A poem is an Anthem
A poem is a Requiem
Pathetic justification

Synctatic didactic climactic
Literary poetry
Read a performance
Perform a reading
Prophetic just is

Jussive entertainment
Narrated and berated
Language arranged
Luingistically changed
Poetic licence
    James Allan

James Allen was born in 1955 in Glasgow. He writes for fun,
for tunes and, hopefully, fortune.

Forever Gone!

I can't stare at the walls anymore,
or look out of the window.
I can't even face the door, and
no more will I pace the floor.
I am leaving - forever.

Life, has no meaning for me,
there is nowhere to go, as I see,
only blackness and emptiness,
nothing fulfilled.
I am leaving - forever.

Will they say I was bad
when I'm gone?
Will they know I was sad
for so long?
Was there help for me then?
there will be none now.
I am better, forever - gone!

I can't stare anymore,
or care anymore.
No tears will come.
In one split second
I am, forever - gone!
   Jennifer Nesbitt

Jennifer Nesbitt was born in Lincolnshire and now lives near
Bath, running her own secretarial business. She has two sons
and is a school governer and church secretary. She writes
poetry for enjoyment.

Remembering

Hazy sun, speckled dew
Misty mornings, rustic hue
Birds migrating, frosty nights,
Crisp leaves falling, winds that bite.
Minds remembering springs fresh blooms
Daffodils, snow drops, brides and grooms.
Seedlings, greeting, blossom bursting,
Weeds peeping, buds thirsting.
Pale blue clear skies,
Fresh smell of hawthorn, bright sunrise.

Minds remembering summer gladness
Barbeques, cycling, sunbathing madness.
T-Shirts, sun cream,
salads and ice cream
Garden teas, car rides,
Picnics and sea-sides.

Chilly mornings, duvet nights,
Weather forecast not so bright.
Woollen jumpers, heavy coats
Search the cupboard for winter boots
Flowers and shrubs drooping with frost
Bright colours fading, beauty lost.
Snow crisp and cold
Covering earths old
Still and silent descending, hiding sleeping roots
Awaiting summer sun to yield it's newborn shoots.
    Cornelia Morton

Cornelia Morton was born In Aberbargoed in 1941. Retired
from nursing in 1987, her hobbies are making celebration
cakes and of course poetry. 'Remembering' is her first
attempt at publication.

Maureen the Socialite

Maureen the Socialite
Wrote a book full of trite
You're not in but don't despair
The day of reckoning's coming near
When you and I and thousands more
Go silently through that golden door
To be ajudged by one who'll know
Who's who! What's what and where we'll go.
And if by chance within that crowd
You hear a voice that cries out loud
'I'm here - you know me well by name'
That wise old man will not refrain
From welcoming with open arms

This socialite with all her charms
So let's be joyful
Do not carp
Maureen's finally found her harp.
  Sheila O'Neill

Sheila O'Neil was born in Dublin, an actress by trade her
main interests are singing and writing for drama and poetry.

A Secret Sadness

Perennial Queen of the Summer Ball, though sad perchance
To be the floral paragon of prim propriety,
Enacts her God-chosen role while other flowers dance.
Yet my red-eyed rose, it seems, longs for their society
And would gladly change her lonely throne for a common
                                                bed
Of a different culture - the more colourful for that -
But good breeding prevents this drastic step, so she instead
Must suffer her isolation, remain disconsolate.
Thus, duty-bound, she bravely smiles through each long year,
The perfect flower: divinely fragrant, forever sweet,
And yet I fear each fallen petal is a heartfelt tear,
And yet I know each sigh will be discreet.

But while I share the secret sadness of her pose
I think how sad would be summer without a rose!
  Roy Allen

Roy Allen, shortly to retire from British Telecom begins a
new career with Safefoam mail order, while being heavily
involved with his grandchildren Joseph, Eleanor and Grace.

Medicine Garden

The apple trees' arms stretch out as if pleading.
They are fixed against the wall.
Espaliers they call them, but are they bleeding?
Do they mind crucifixion, do they mind at all?

Poppies thrust through broken stones
To beckon with their opium sleep.
Foxgloves, digitalis, attacks on hearts postpones.
Hemlock, like the part of us that's schizoid
Surely warns us to avoid
All contact with it, and keep our own counsel
Wisely cultivating the yellow groundsel
So that we can make a poultice
Healing as a summer solstice.
   Peggy Trott

The Human Monster

The crowd gathered around
As the curtain unveiled
And they gasped when they saw
The thing in the cage,
It was small and hunched
And gripped the cage with puny hands,
The people stood back
As it let out a high pitched squeal
From it's black-lipped mouth,
And it looked at them
Through yellow eyes,
The showman offered eggs and tomatoes
And said 'Hide it's scabby face'.
The thing touched his scabs
Which engulfed his face
And cowered back as the food hit him,
And it cried, 'stop them father.'
But the showman ignored him.
   Lee Brown

Lee Brown is currently a student teacher at Charlotte Mason College in Ambleside. He has had some of his work published in magazines and has also appeared in another anthology.

Twilight

Twilight is the most precious
Part of our day,
All harsh thoughts are softened,
And beauty shows her curved cheek
To the velvet night
In supple surrender.

At moments such as these
Our seeing eyes are dimmed,
As grey drifts of dust
Clinging like soft drapes surround us,
And the perfumed breath of earth
Hovers vacant in still air.
   Elizabeth Mathers

Elizabeth Mathers is a retired nurse, married to a police officer, living in Fylde. Her hobbies include poetry, fell-walking and flower pressing.

The Briefcase of Dorian Grey

It was the briefcase I noticed first;
Gleaming crocodile, gold-monogrammed,
Fort-Knox-combination-locked,
It dangled from the elegantly manicured hand
Of a lady commuter on the 7.22.

Alighting from her Thameslink carriage,
She strutted down the station platform,
Smugly aware of the envious glances
Of the less well-dressed female passengers.

Her pink silk designer jacket, immaculately tailored,
And the black silk skirt swirling around her calves
Would have kept us in groceries for a month;
Her shoes would have paid our gas bill.

But as she left the station forecourt
And headed for the local taxis
Her image wavered and dissolved in the twilight
Like a desert mirage in the Saturday movies.

I rubbed my eyes and looked at her again
And saw a tired, heavy middle-aged woman
With bleeding lipstick and smudged mascara
Whose shoes pinched, whose girdle was too tight,

And whose briefcase had become a wastebin
Full of sandwich crumbs, shattered illusions
And old, unanswered, loveletters.
    Leonie Aldridge

Leonie Aldridge became a performing poet when she was
old enough to know better. A West London resident, she is
red-haired, tattooed and bad tempered, and currently seeks
a publisher for her first collection of poems.

A Lifetime in a Year

I remember early spring,
School days, games and swings.
Carefree days filled with promises,
Happy days with no time to spare.
Later in spring, promises fade away
Like flowers do always.
Early summer new responsibilities.
I reasses my priorities,
New hopes, new dreams.
Some are fulfilled some are unreal.
I wished for so much
I got much more than I wished for.

Now in September, I don't remember,
My dreams, my desires, my hopes.
I thank God for all I have
And for all I have had,
And with His blessing
Winter will be like springtime,
With so much to do and not enough time.
And when winter meets spring,
It will be a complete ring
And I, nothing.
   Lucia Fella

Lucia Iafano Fella came to Leeds from Italy in 1966, not
knowing a word of English. To improve her written English
she began to write verses. Today she simply writes for
pleasure.

Wing

Coy ghosts of blinds
Peer through glass -
gatecrashing sweetbriar
patches holes in stone.

From underwing
Your babes are flown -
- you'd not be amused
by the slapbrick nursery

where fathers are
Welcomed day or night.
(you banished men to
a Smoking Room or

out to gardens where
pale narcissi grew
in regimental beds)

Under your wing
each swaddled child
- patted and petted,
New mothers you mothered
(Like your own)

We waited at gates,
with our nervous charges,
as you called out
'See you next year...next year...next year...?
  L. Liffen

Lorna Liffen lives in London and is a cleaning supervisor
working on her own collection of poetry.

Daddy's Darling

'They'll never belive you' he whispers seductively,
Smug in his felony, bullying soft.
She knows he is right, so she stares at her film stars,
Not seeing, but nothing can shut out the pain.

A useful appliance, he fills her to tearstains,
A pillow to smother the screams that burst free.
Her freedom is emptiness, sticky and painful,
He kisses her forehead and smoothes back her hair,

Then leaves her alone with the actress inside her,
Rehearsing her smile for the spotlight of day
He returns, dripping, to mummy and slumber,
She squirms with dirtiness, deep as the thrust.

He told her he loved her, then shoved her through torment;
A paradox innocence can't understand.
As dawn creeps home slyly, she works our excuses;
A bad dream for supper, but really she's fine.

The man makes a joke of the fools who befriend him,
A whore of his daughter who never gets paid;
Her luggage goes noticed, she lies to protect him,
And blinks back the breakdown, then walls up her eyes.

'They'll never believe you' he whispers to stifle her,
Knowing she knows they will call her a liar.
A reinforced nightmare, but false as his values;
She's a time-bomb of secrets and Daddy's best girl.
    Anthony J. Fyler

Anthony Fyler was born in Merthyr Tydfil, South wales in
1971. He is studying law at Southampton University and
intends eventually to enter the House of Commons. He hopes
to publish his first collection shortly.

The Arrival

The creaky door opened ajar
A scruffy man walked from afar
A new arrival I heard them say

Unwashed and unshaven
He looked quite a sight
To pry off his coat
With all of our might

Eyes very sullen
A bottle in hand
Why was he a tramp
They did not understand
    Mark Pettet

Mark Pettet was born in 1965 in Erith. He has been writing
for the last few years where he now lives, in Bexley Heath.
His interests are art, music, photography and extensive
reading. He hopes to have a slim volume of work published.

A Winter Sky

As I looked at that sky, that deep dark night
Self-illuminated only, no town lamp bright
To dim the majesty of it, no cloud
To obscure a single star, I was allowed
To pierce great heaven with my wond'ring gaze
And marvel at it's deep galactic ways.
Not since my boyhood had I been so fired
With rapt amazement, nor yet admired
Its far immensity. Words came not then;
I could not form the thoughts that tumble here
So overcome was I. Was it great fear
Of understanding an enormity
I do now see - how very small are we?
   R. M. Stephens

Roger Stephens is a primary school Headteacher in
Oxfordshire. Born in 1940, he has been writing poetry as a
means of relaxation for ten years but has only now offered
his work for publication.

Cricket

I loved those long and leafy afternoons
of leisure, leaning at the cricket green,
lost in meditation, drifting between
the hours and the tinkling teaspoons,
endlessly listening to the easy tunes
of wood on willow, as time has been
arrested: oblivious of the unseen
shadows, I dreamed away those sleepy Junes.
Life is like that: there, the livelong day
they toss and pitch their talents; here, I,
absorbed in the game and the current fray,
forget the wickets falling steadily
till it's too late for me to join the play,
for now the time to act has passed away.
   D. W. Fincham

D. W. Fincham is a school teacher who works in Wimbledon. In his spare time he likes reading, listening to music and watching sport. He is married with three children.

An Old Fashioned Christmas

An old fashioned Christmas, with old fashioned ways,
laughter and happiness, and families to stay,
Old ones, young ones, and friends we know well,
To the sound of the old church bells.

It is time for rejoicing, a time full of cheer,
To carry us through, an unknown New year,
Puddings are steaming, mince pies are baking,
Old fashioned mulled wine we will be partaking.
So put up the chains and tinsel and the tree,
There is plenty to eat for you and me
Yet wait, what of the ones who are hungry and cold,
Especially alone, those who are young and old,
Shall they go without, that are out of the fold?
No! Not while there is a God in Heaven above,
We will spread his bounteous love,
So dig in your pockets, your larders and coal,
Let the good tidings and happiness roll.
We come with gifts and our presents for you,
With love in our hearts, and the Christ child too,
For lo, it is his Birthday that we celebrate,
God bless our Christmas bake.

Alas, there are some, who will never come home,
From which they never wanted to roam,
God bless all the people, who will never see,
The lighted candles on a Christmas tree.
So rejoice for the babe born in Bethlehem,
For we can never know how or when,
Jesus will come to save us again,
From wars and famine, grief and pain,
God bless our old fashioned Christmas.
  Elizabeth R. Jordan

Elizabeth R. Jordan lives in London, now retired from the bakery she likes writing poetry, laments and short stories.

I Am Witch

While I'm burning I've something to tell
About good people I scream and I yell
the flames creeping higher, my body it fries
Oh you good people are you deaf to my cries.

Somebody accused me, I fled from the town.
I knew it wouldn't take long for them tracking me down
and now I'm burning I curse holy men
and curse them and curse them 'til hell freezes in.

And they damned me, said I was a witch
Witch hunters followed me here
and they stripped me, poked me with pins
For good people all filled with fear.

They asked me questions, pulled at my nails
They broke my body but my spirit was strong
kept turning the thumbscrews, I cried out to God
but they wouldn't believe they could ever be wrong.

And then my mind went and I said
'I Am Witch'.
Witch hunters they are to blame
'The devil take them, please God forsake them'
Are the last words I screamed through the flames.
    Peter Glasgow

Peter Glasgow is an exiled Londoner living in Exeter. He has been writing poetry for many years and is waiting to be discovered.

Shall We Find Friends?

Out there in space shall we find friends
Mankind needs a place to make his amends.
Can Destiny lead us to live by God's laws?
Freedom from tyrants and void of all wars.

Can we find peace way out there in space
Before the destruction of all human race?
Can life be humble? Can there lie a way
Where the future is planned for an age not a day?

Out there in space on some distant star
Can we go forward - not stand as we are?
Where the future is free for people to share
And the past is a memory treasured with care.

For in the heavens is there such a place
Unspoiled by religion or hatred of race
Where life can begin and start all anew
Where your word is your bond and all values are true

Where terror and hunger and greed are unknown
And each one's a friend and none walks alone
Where each man's burden is shared by his friend
And tolerance and justice shine through to the end.

Out there in space shall we find friends?
Is Paradise found where the universe ends?
Can peace in a garden of Eden remain
Will the cycle on earth start all over again?
　　D. Payne

Derek Payne lives in Stevenage and has written poetry for
friends and personal pleasure for over thirty years. One day
he may try to have it published.

In This Room

In this room we talked
And the words came tumbling out
Racing; falling over one another
As if to relieve the pressure,
Pushed up against our chests

In this room we cried, as we tried
To piece together the shattered fragments
Of a broken relationship
To show each other, through tears and words
That it wasn't how we each thought it was

In this room we laughed, albeit nervously,
And the eagerness began to show through
That it was a mutual want to begin again

In this room we lingered, not wanting to push away
Or be the first to move,
Less the other think it didn't
Mean as much to him.
   Steve O'Hara

Steve O'Hara lives in Manchester. He attended Loughborough
University and is at present a teacher in special education.

Postman Fred

I hear those footsteps again; familiar in sound as the rhythm
                                     of my heartbeat.
Our postman is garbed in smart navy blue; a bringer of
                                           tidings.
Today, he carries another neat bundle of secrets, hidden in
                                   sealed envelopes.
Large and small; assorted colours.

There's five birthday cards for little Sarah, who is three
                                                        today,
A 'get well' card for Bertie, the pensioner, who lives next
                                                        door.
And Olive Brown, opposite, receives her telephone bill from
                                                        'BT'

Could someone from somewhere unfold their feelings and
                                                write to me?
I would like to hear my letterbox click again.
Fred won't mind.
     Minnie Fenton

Minnie Fenton is a retired youth worker who has had short
articles published in local newspapers. Her hobbies include
painting in watercolour and charity work. She hopes to
compile a collection of poetry soon. Minnie was born in
London.

Sunday Morning

Strolling along a footpath fields so white
Frosted hedge trees glitter bright
Passing a cowshed a farmyard smell
Bit of rural England I can tell

Leaving their houses in the square
Worshippers to church, their weekly prayer
Church tower clock strikes half ten
Verger looks out now and then

All Saints Church bell ringing
Organist plays while pews are filling
Stained windows magnificent sight
By morning sunbeams shining bright

From the altar, Vicar leads in prayer
The poor, the sick, we must care
Collection plate passed for donation
Choir sings to the congregation

Service ends, meet the vicar outside
For your guidance he will oblige
Winter's hard frost takes a grip
Sunday morning, care not to slip.
   Frank Prosser

Frank Prosser is a retired railwayman, born in 1916 in
Chatham, Kent, he started writing at the age of seventy
two about his forty six years experience in St. John
Ambulance. A year later he began writing poems.

My Greatest Pleasure

I leave the clubhouse like a giant,
I'm proud and dressed to kill,
My caddie smiles, I nod and take a stimulatory pill.
I swing in practice like a dream, my name should be Sam
                                       Snead,
But when I hit my drive, it's like the ball was never tee'ed.
I'm hooking and I'm slicing but play well from the rough,
My hair and clothes are full of sand, these bunker shots are
                                       tough.
My cabbie doesn't like me, he clubs me short each green
I heard him whisper loudly, 'This guy plays like a queen.'
He looks straight down the fairway, each time I lose my
                                       ball,
And when it struck the Captain, my caddie didn't call.
By now I'm on the thirteenth tee, with only six to play
If I can get five birdies, I'll still lose anyway.
So now I hand four fivers to my slow swinging friend
And leave the course a broken man, I wish the world would
                                       end.

   Tony Booth

Tony Booth writes poems and songs and is now working on his first novel. He won the Songwriters Guild Contest in 1963, and has had several poems published. He is also a golf addict.

Thoughts on Carvings on the Walls of an Old Building

Deep in this stone is carved a name.
Perhaps some long dead hand had sought
A tenuous immortality,
And, striving to acheive the fame
That life witheld from him, he caught
A fleeting joy that there should be
Somewhere this sign for all to see.
And comforted himself that 'He
Who finds this mark, will know I came.
To some part of eternity
With chisel I will stake a claim'
John Henry, Eighteen Fifty Three
   Anne Hetherton

Anne Hetherton was born in Sheffield in 1920 and now lives in the country near York, surrounded by family and an assortment of animals.

Untitled

'Life is just a one way street.'
Is one school of contention.
'The Road to Hell', some others say,
'Is paved with good intention.'
With streets and roads and highways long,
The path of life is clear.
But life is nought along this route,
With no one to hold dear.

'With worldly goods I thee endow',
Are words we all know well.
But with these goods, go other things,
Things we cannot buy and sell.
'To have loved and lost', the maxim goes,
'Tis like a Clarion call.
'To have loved and lost, far better be,
Than to not have loved at all'.

Having lived my life, some fifty years
And filled up every second.
Been led astray, been sad, been gay,
Refused when temptation beckoned.
Through all the laughter, joys and tears,
No stronger feelings ran.
With all his frailties and fears,
A caring, human, wondrous being
He is my fellow man!
   Brian J. Harris

Brian Harris is a professional engineer who loves writing and
painting in oils.

I Took Little Emma

Walking along the high street every face seemed sad,
Every heart seemed sad, every soul was sad.
All were pulling or pushing baskets of nothing with Maryanne
and I too became sad, with a dread, prophetic sadness.

So I took little Emma away from that high street,
away on a tup'ny tube to the Common of Clapham.
We bought a chocolate ice, threw grass at each other,
and watched the ducks quacking along a shimmering pond.
Emma's face and heart laughing, making laughter with her
                                      eyes

How strange, a world where only a child can laugh,
Thinking this I kissed her, burying her lovely face,
Smothering her golden hair in the jacket of my best.
When, from a lifeless sky they dropped a bomb,
And thy child rocked, rocked with unending laughter.
    Laurence Smith

Laurence Smith was born in the North of England in 1918.
He went to sea at 14, a kind of rebel. His poems were read
around Soho during the 50's and 60's, and despite emphesyma
he still writes today.

The Weeping World

You can't see what I can see,
the future degradation.
The turmoil and the tragedy,
nationwide condemnation.
Our rewards, someone else is reaping,
while we watch our children weeping.
Telling us that all is good
as they draw on our blood.
Squeezing bones for one last drop
to make sure they stay on top.
Unless we rise and all join hands,
they'll leave us with just barren lands.
With the future remaining unwritten,
we must stop those, who by greed, are smitten.
    Russell Ede

Russell Ede is 22 years of age and lives in Sutton, Surrey.
He is a locksmith by trade and only writes as a hobby.

Waltzing With Shadows

See how our shadows dance before our eyes,
Making us laugh with shallow breath and lies;
And in the flick'ring light see how they move,
Waltzing to life as the fire shoots up and dies.

When logical morning rises and shouts,
'Move from your bed and let the day begin!'
Fly from her words as though they were the dream;
Sieze your souls and flee from her lecturing.

We were not born to march but born to live;
Love like the heroes, strong in word and song;
Act like myths and create them in our wake -
Not watch our shadows dance through life alone.
    Louise Fish

Louise Fish is a twenty one year old secretary who lives
in Epsom. She has been writing poems and stories since she
was four years old.

Odious Man

You, squalid man
It is your very form that mocks the shadows
of our city lights
And your haggard features, betray indignity
to all that came before
You, beggarman of still-life, with your brown fragmented
teeth and eyes of pallid wax
You squat in hovels of cardboard and disease.
You look from nothing. You are nothing. Just faces
staring into space
A brotherhood despaired, and of human waste.
Your liquor-languid flesh desecrates the very
ground - is all hope lost, and nothing there be found
but a shell, where people died so long ago.

You are the litter of the city streets, that no-one
claims and no one cares
You tattered, match-stick man of no abode, with
odour rancid, and so cold
You have nothing. You want nothing.
You smell of spirit and decay, and will surely
give addiction to the worms and maggots, who will like
you not, nor thank you for your pickled flesh.

And if you now walk in scorn, was it by choice that
you are alone
For what do I recognize in thee, Fagin man. Did
I know you once, those many years ago?
Is this, all, that is left of your candle of life,
that now quivers and flickers on a dry and dying stem
And death is but a blow away.

Is it with pity, that now I ask your name
and sought you in shadow, and shout in whisper
to hide my shame.
Who are you? Old man, your life now spent, that
I should hold you in such contempt
And then I looked into your face, and cried.
For then I knew. For then I knew.
There, in the grace of God, walked I
For then I knew that I was you, and you, old man,
was I.
    Thomas Quiller

Thomas Quiller was born in Scotland of French parentage. He
writes adventure and occult fiction novels as well as poetry.

Aftermath

Flesh revolves and reflects earthly pleasures,
encased in glass, protected from nil.
Empty skulls floating across permanent blue,
drifting slowly to Australia.
You can't see the brown earth, it's covered in algae,

but beneath the suffocation the insects sleep and dream.
Communism has not been born down there.
No choking gas envelopes the freedom,
straitjackets do not exist in the world of the free.
But who are you?
Walking on pavements still damp from the previous
nights fallout.
Souls that tried to escape lay rotting in caves,
stalactites are no longer there, the labour of a thousand
years destroyed in one second of fanatical pleasure.
The trees which once breathed life gain new friendship
with their gnarled neighbours.
The hills are barren, scorched by the blast,
But the molten earth deep beneath growls in defiance,
yielding not to the Master who wears an iron gauntlet.
But the rains will lash and the winds corrode, and time,
to decay the glove.
The earth will awaken, pushing forth fingers of life;
first a trickle,
gaining strength until it blossoms into a rushing torrent!
Tiny green shoots appear through the blackened soil.
Buds cautiously peer at the sky;
sky purified of evil.
The first song of a bird drifts through the unblemished air,
and a baby is born!
Around it's neck is tied a label and on it written;
PITY ME!
    Brian Denton

Brian Denton was born in Stockport, Cheshire and now lives
in London. He has written poetry for many years but this
is his first poem to be published.

The Otter

The flash of white water, the swirl of a tail,
the sight of the Otter at play
The greatest of swimmers, the masterman fisher,
But have you seen one today.

Like the fox they were hunted and killed for their sport,
So wrongly considered a pest
But for sheer excitement and joy of life
The Otter is always the best.

The slaughter was stopped before we were born
Yet the Otter is rare in our land
And the state of our waters will not aid its plight
That is why we must all make a stand -

To make our world safer and cleaner
for all that share with us in life
Then the Otter, Elephant, Rhino and Whale
will be saved from the torment and strife.

To excite all our children and show us each day,
the flash of white water, the Otter at play.
  Mark Wetherby

Mark Wetherby was born in Banbury, Oxfordshire in 1948.
He is a former journalist who has written several poems and
children's books and is looking forward to publishing them
under his own imprint in the future.

The Unexpected Guest

He arrived,
As unexpected as raindrops in the Sahara,
Old for his nineteen years
He was a young boy,
Chubby-cheeked, freckled, straight from cricket practice as

They invited him to fight for his country
And changed him to a man, hardened by war
With a mind full of horrors.

Those who hadn't seen, couldn't imagine.

He flinched as she hugged him;
Repressed memories emerging of comrades
Dying in those arms now around her.
She sensed the change
And sat quiet as they laid him
A place at the table;
Parents rejoicing among thousands who mourned
The loss of their sons.
That night, nightmares which had been real
Returned to plague him as illusions.
He cried in her arms
As men had done in his.

He felt a guest in his own home
Being treated specially because he was there:
But it hadn't been a party
And he was tired of comments
Telling of how brave he was
At the party where he had been
An unexpected guest.
   Emma Williams

Emma Williams is a final year student at Bristol University.
She is the daughter of Peter Williams who also has a poem
in this book.

Me

I started life a daughter,
Alas an only child
I never was called sister
I'd have driven a brother wild
Aunties said I was their niece
Uncles said it too
I also was called cousin
But only by a few
I then became a student
A friend and colleague too
A girl-friend and a sweetheart
But don't tell 'you know who'
I loved being called fiance
And wife was a dream come true
I too became daughter and sister-in-law
I quite like those names too
The impending patter of little feet
Meant my next name would be Mom
A name to surpass all others
A job till kingdom come
Today I became a mother-in-law
As my young son takes a bride
And may I say right here and now
I take the name with pride
There's only one name more for me
Guess it if you can
I look to my son and daughter-in-law
For my final name of Nan.
　　Margaret Reardon

Margaret Reardon is school secretary at a primary school
in Birmingham. She enjoys writing poetry, particularly for
special occasions. This is the first time her work has been
published.

Alone

And now he is gone,
no longer a part of my life.
Yes, he is here still
But no longer shall I see the twinkle
in his eyes that was known only to us;
The unseen brush of his body against mine
when we were not just two;
No longer shall we laugh,
at secret, childish jokes.
Were it not for her, we would be one.
How I despise her
Her that took away my Greek God.
She who is like an invisible wall,
Forever separating us from what we want.
Why should time strengthen his feelings
for her and not me?
We had only seven days and nights;
they passed like the blink of an eye
But, they were good, they were heavenly.
Why can she not free her captive to me
and enmesh someone worthy of herself?
Not one who she keeps by female tricks.
    Simone A. F. McEvoy-Morris

Simone McEvoy-Morris was born in England in 1972, the
daughter of an English father and Irish mother. She moved
with her family to live in her mothers home town, Dundalk,
in the Republic of Ireland.

Interview

Rejection! Slap hits cheek,
Head swivels immediately,
Mouth smiles prettily
As other cheek meets slap.

Victim of verbal abuse,
Interview door locked;
Attack, defend, attack, half-defend,
Attack, withdraw.

Final boot in the stomach
As you pick yourself off the floor
'Thank you,' so nicely, 'for coming.
We'll be back in touch for some more.'

Rejection!
Letter slides gently through the door.
  Deborah Davis

Deborah Davis was born in 1959 and lives with her family in Hertfordshire.

The Graveyard

Ghost's creeping round in the middle of the night
In the dark, dark graveyard, they'll give you a fright
Boo!
A skeleton gets up from his grave
To go there, you must be very brave.
Boo!

Zombies and banshees they all creep around
And there's a rat scuttling on the ground
Boo!
The Devil laughs with his red, red eyes
The banshee wails and the banshee cries.
Boo!

The mummy's wrapped in strips of cloth
You must not sneeze and you must not cough
Boo!
A witch is making up a spell
She'll not go to heaven, but she will go to hell.
Boo!

Lot's of people are buried here
They died of fright and they died with fear
Boo!
Now the dawn is breaking, the spooks have gone to bed
So no more stories of the evil, gruesome dead!
Boo!
   Louise Liszewski

Louise Liszewski is a Christmas baby, born on Boxing Day in 1979. She enjoys writing poems and short stories.

Untroubled Waters

Sit awhile on my golden lawn
Watch my roaring entrance
Bringing nothing
But my soothing tide

Immerse in my silence
Between my gossiping surges
Listening I lay at your feet
Pass to me your troubles
Far, so far away I will take them

Stand awhile and gaze
I am forever
Ease in my soothing grasp
Years sped on, people change
I don't alter
My return is sure

A clear open mind
That is all I bring
Feel, look, cherish
Inhale my aroma
Peace, mystery and calmness descend

Go now if you must
Back to society's clasp
But remember this time
As troubles abound
My roar, my trickle
Seagulls crying
A ship is calling
Quick, catch the serenity
Come back, come back
I will
   Shane White

Shane White was born in Ireland and now lives in
Buckinghamshire. He is currently writing a book on South
Armagh.

The Glad and Sad of Winter

The first snow of winter has coated the land
An army of snowmen are moulded by hand
Dressed up in boots; old scarf and tattered coat
So well-dressed it makes one gloat!

Silent and fearless; they stand and stare
Everything they survey is lifeless and bare
With two coals for eyes and a carrot nose
A smiling face with twig arms and toes

What can we learn from these men of snow
Perhaps that life comes and goes
What will happen when the winter sun appears?
Melted men and children's tears.
   Alison E. Johnson

Alison E. Johnson was born in Edinburgh in 1973 and now lives in Wormit, Fife. She is a student nurse at a local hospital and enjoys writing, dancing, sports and travelling.

Junkie

Yet again I clasp the cold dead hand of night,
and find no solace in the swift descending gloom,.
As I seek to oust the world 'til morning light,
the shadows dance obscenely round my cluttered room.

I beg thee return demented thoughts to all those virgin years
Of Christmases, birthdays; and a Love freely gave.
In a loving world I closed my heart to family tears
and unrepenting scorned the friendly hand to save.

What ails this joyous cloud of dreams? A peak where many
                                                    climb.
We crowd these wretched heights, so why should it demean
our weak unhesitating cry? We can kick this habit any time.
so is it just be chance you came upon this tawdry scene?

A junkie still I live for yet another day
you stand there disapproving, ill-at-ease.
Is it you I spurn and turn away?
When deep inside my soul a silent voice is calling;
Help me, help me, please.
    Eddy Plummer

Eddy Plummer was born in Bramford, near Ipswich in 1923. An ex-Royal Marine. Married and settled near Goodrington in Devon. A member of 'Arvon Writers' he contibutes to magazines and has had his poems broadcast on radio.

Drunk with Poppies

Drunk with poppies
The long grasses,
your lashes.
The splash of red,
Lips, I kiss
Rising up to meet me
in the first blush of light.

Drunk with poppies
Butterfly land,
the flutterby of your hand.
The gentle whishing and
swaying.
In the gust of grace
your body inclined.

So very drunk with poppies
full blown
in love.
   Polly High

Polly High, artist and poet, born in 1962, lives in London and on the Kent coast. Some of her work has been published in various poetry periodicals.

Untitled

Was it passion
Of a fashion
The first time?

Was it need
Or just greed
Or thirst time?

Or was it more
An open door
From the worst time?

Or was it us
With no fuss
Falling in love?
   Katy Plant

Katy Plant lives in Marketr Harborough, works in sales and
hopes to publish a first collection shortly.

Silverdale Pit

The pit we know is not too nice,
It's dark and it's deep and one or two mice,
It takes a man to work the pit,
Not a fool or an idiot.

Each workman here holds an ace,
He puts things down in the proper place,
A bar, a post, a pick or nail,
Don't leave it lying across the rail.

Move it now we must insist,
Don't leave it for the other shift,
A friend of yours might fall on it,
Right on his face into the pit,

You can change that verse a little bit,
Change the word pit (to shit),
If you do this, then I have done my best,
If you remember this then you will remember the rest.
   S. D. Robinson

Stanley Derek Robinson lives in Silverdale, Newcastle, Staffs.
He was born in 1938 and is a general engineer. He hopes
to have more work published in the future as he has been
writing poetry since 1962.

A Winters Storm

A blazing fire we sit beside
As it is damp and cold outside
The sky is heavy, dull and grey
It is a rather dismal day
The cat is curled up on the rug
As we all sit nice and snug
A flash of lightning lights the room
Then we hear a very loud boom
The heavens open, down comes the rain
Beating hard on the window pane
Then it started to subside
We began to look outside
In the sky there is a rainbow beam
Everywhere is so fresh and clean
All is quiet and very calm
After we have had this winter storm.
   Maybrill Lee

Maybrill Lee is a housewife, mother and grandmother. She is employed part-time in the food industry, and she enjoys writing poetry.

Seasons

She wakes with him in the brightness of the morning
The birds break the silence with their song of spring
Brave young flowers intrude through the bleak soil
And the sun is warm, falling into the room upon her face
Unexpected showers will dampen her hair
As they run, hand in hand, together

She strolls with him on this hazy afternoon
Through golden fields of corn, to the river's edge
Here they will bathe naked in the cool summer water

And they will lay in the tall grass until dusk leads them
home
Freshly cut grass will collect in her hair
As they run, hand in hand, together

She walks with him in the quiet of the evening
Through the skeleton of trees the sun fades in the distance
She hides and he searches, softly calling her name
And she laughs as she catches him unaware
Autumn leaves will cling to her hair
As they run, hand in hand, together

She sits with him in the stillness of the night
As the winter moon steals a pathway across the window
Watching the snowflakes fall into their footsteps
The solitary snowman grins his coal smile
As dancing flames reflect in her eyes
As they lay, hand in hand, together
    Alison Culpeck

Alison Culpeck is 28 and lives in London. She writes poetry
as a hobby, although is hoping for more of her work to be
published.

Free

When I was down
And on my knees
Oh yes my Lord
You heard my pleas

When I was in
The dark of night
You came and helped
To shine the light

When I was in
The depths of sadness
Oh yes my Lord
You brought me gladness

When I was in
My days of pain
Oh yes my Lord
You helped me again

When I was told
There is nothing free
How they were wrong
You charge no fee
   Bobby Evans

Bobby Evans was born in 1949 in Banbridge, Co. Down. He
is a games designer for newspaper games, working on TV
formats for quiz shows and would like to write a book.

Crisis

Your heart is aching, your mouth feels dry,
You're trying not to but you have to cry,
You touch his hand laying on the bed
Stroke his cheek, feel his head,
Please don't go you want to say,
I love you dearly and come what may,
I'll always be there by your side,
To help you rebuild your crumbled life.

For hours you sit so still and forlorn,
Studying his quiet lifeless form,
Willing with all your heart and might,
That he will make it through the night,
The crisis comes as dawn is breaking,
The birds their joyous songs are making,
The sky so beautiful to see, slowly fades,
As at long last life returns from whence it past,

His fingers pressed your cold white hand,
Asking you to understand that your
Mother love has pulled him through,
And with your help he'll start anew.
  Valerie Helliar

Valerie Helliar lives in Southend-on-Sea, she works full time
for a well known charity and this is the first of her poems
to be published.

Poem for a New year

These windblown leaves of my mind,
Caught by chance and gathered,
I send as wandering words
Penned in uncertain lines for you
At the ending of another year
And though the distant sounds of summer
Fade like voices in the wind,
Memories of days like flowers
Still fill the corners of my mind.
Now in the winter of the year
I find myself with scrambled thoughts
Seeking elusive words like 'share'
And 'love' and 'touch' and 'close'
And complicated phrases like 'your eyes'.
That leaves have fallen from my mind
And lie at random for you to find.
  Geoffrey Scott Houghton

Geoffrey Scott Houghton was for many years a school
teacher before giving this up to concentrate on freelance
journalism and writing. He has never previously submitted
his work for publication.

Untitled

Don't you come huffily stubble to me
with your overcoat depressions;
furrowed brows winking at the brim
of a hat.

You bore me
with your hands-deep-in-pocket thoughts;
hole-in-shoe-shuffle with sad old seg sound.

Your turn-ups tell tale of turn downs.
You escape for a while through the neck
of a good second-hand shirt.

Ritzy jackets, razzy ties;
belted-up trousers strain
over circuit-trained thighs.

You want to be in a boom town baby
...so go.
 Joan Borland

Joan Borland was born in Glasgow in 1960. She rarely
submits her work for publication and is pleased to see her
first published poem in this anthology. It has inspired her
to try harder to get more of her work published.

The Dreaming Mouth

The dreaming mouth, taking in food and wine between
          talking,
Your mouth that could begin to touch each of your fingers
In miracles of transgression, no one realising;
Glass ordinary; all arrayed,
The cutlery staying layed in it's prizons of silver.
 David Johnson

David Johnson is 26 and lives in Leicestershire. He has been published in several anthologies and is a student of literature and Philosophy.

Winter

Life, like the weather has it's seasons,
Spring, summer, autumn and wintertime
Every season has it's blessings
Not always does the sun brightly shine.
Spring - when all if young and gay,
Happiness, fun and joy grow strong
Time to learn, to play and work
Small tasks of life sometimes to shirk.
Summer - like the sunshine,
Warm glows many a heart,
With a partner to cherish and love
Joined in marriage, never to part.
The autumn years fly quickly by
Time for reflection, freedom and pleasure,
Toils which for years have been a burden
Now bring ease and happiness - such treasure.
Winter when the limbs feel tired and weary
The eyes grow dim - often bleary.
For me, my wintertime is half way through
Each new day thankfully I've learnt to live anew.
Keep me dear Lord not cold and bare
Frosty, like a winter morn,
As was the cold March day when I was born
Happy each day the new dawn to see
Until you call 'come, come home to me'
Come to my home, I have promised for you
After the cold grey days of winter are through.
   G. M. Hawthorn

Gladys Hawthorn is in the winter of her life, a spinster, alone yet never alone. Only latterly has she begun writing poems or remembrances, it gives her great comfort and happy memories.

A Mushroom for Chris

Our deaths should not find us alone
In our gaze, the land's wide curve sways
As a quilt of fields on a hammock horizon.

Nor should the ocean's expanse dwarf our last sail
While sour grey waters lap, hungry to devour,
Without guilt, the flamed pyre our black corpse lies on.

Living with ourselves, shadows are forces
Breathing old doubts when music pauses
And we wilt, sadly, as the song cries on.

This fear, to die friendless, haunts me too.
I shall not go easy, so I pursue
To the hilt, each dream, each cloud to rise on.

And did once I see, beneath your dark fringe,
This reflection deep in your soul? All this truth,
Gently built, was there, yes. And how your eyes shone!
   H. John Percival

John Percival, company director, is a former chairman of
the Granville Writers' Circle. He has coached drama locally,
had three of his plays performed locally and has completed
his first publication of songs.

Dreams

Sometimes I like to sit and dream
Of things I'd love to do
I travel the exotic lands
Where skies are always blue.

I climb the highest mountains
And explore unchartered seas
And life is just an endless round
Of doing as I please.

I own a splendid mansion
In a green and pleasant land
With slaves to do my bidding
At the raising of a hand.

But dreams must end and life begin
And I can clearly see
That all the things I treasure most
I have right here with me.

No doubt I'll go on dreaming,
And I'll feel the urge to roam
But deep within my heart I know
There's no place quite like home.
    Alfreda Edna Jones

Freda Jones is a housewife whose retirement has given her
opportunity to indulge in her passion for poetry, and to
branch out into writing short verses of her own.

To Care For Me

When you walk by and maybe see
A casual glance or smile from me,
Try to realise that in my way
I do appreciate what you do and say,
You are young and your life is new,
You are agile, pretty and gay,
But of life's experiences you know little
The youthful years are to be desired,
We learn as we pass through each phase,
We laugh, we sigh, we remember,
We talk and dream of love,
Make the most of all you have,
And enjoy life to the full,
But may I gently say to you,
That all this I have done,

And this old lady that you see,
Has done all this and more,
When I am tired and feeling low,
My memories keep me young,
And bear in mind,
When you are old,
My thoughts will be your own
    Joy Alford

Joy Alford was born in Bournemouth and hopes to have more work published.

Heartbroken

People will look and say I'm heartbroken
But not a word to me have they spoken
They will look sorry but still they stare
You see my child is handicapped he sits in a chair
At first my husband he took it quite well
But now he's withdrawn into a shell
He wants our son placed in a home
I can't stand it, I'm helpless I feel all alone
I try so hard but my feelings must show
I love him so much I can't let him go
His hair is so curly and he's very fair
Why did God give me this burden to bear
I love my husband with all my heart
But there is just no way out, we just have to part
When my husband looks at him, he sheds silent tears
He looks so much older than his thirty years
Oh please help me, someone please hear my cry
There are somedays I just wish I could die.
    George F. Main

Reflections

In a glass darkly
the image I see,
is the child of the woman
that's lost inside me.

Childhood of innocence
So freely spent
Soon left to wonder
Where sweet childhood went.

Many decades passing
a fickle friend is time
Soon left to wonder
were the memories really mine.

For as time is passing
So must our youth
and the lessen it teaches
is facing the truth,

In a glass darkly
the image I see
is the child in the woman
that longs to be free:
   Lesley Scott

Lesley Scott, born in London in 1950, now living in
Buckinghamshire, has been writing poetry since early
adolescence, reflections is the first of her poems to be
published.

Homesick

Why did we have to leave our native land
We were forced by Maggie Thatcher's hand
She bled our little business dry
and I still wonder why oh why

The first five years were very good
We sold drinks and lovely food
Unemployment affected our customers very bad
and for our trade this was very bad
The bills came in but the money did not
and you can't pay what you ain't got
So we sold out at quite a loss
It's hard not being your own boss
It's most degrading signing on at the dole
We were self employed no money, your back in a hole
No social security, now that's really a joke
When you see all the foreigners collecting their poke
It does not pay to be honest I feel
and Maggie's way of working doesn't seem real
If your alcoholic or a waster I'll be bound
She will give you money to get you off the ground
but if you have worked hard all of your life
All she will give you in the back is a knife
We were proud to be British and that is true
So it's only natural at times we feel blue
and where we are we live quite grand
But still it is a foreign land.
  Anne C. Main

Confusion

Staring into space; turning inwards on myself
Weaving in and out and in again
Through confusion.

Optimism and pessimism, hope and failure,
White and black, light and shade
Become as one and turn to grey.
Grey matter. No matter.

One phase passing through and over
Into the next and back again.
Tossing and turning - to and fro
Swimming against the current, turning against

The tide of life. Then submission carries me
To the shore to settle, to merge with the sand,
To go with the grain.
Sensibility takes me by the hair and
Sits me at the front.
Conformity guides me.
But that desert island continues to tempt me
With it's green and fertile land;
A land that beckons me with it's warmth and ripe
Heart.

Could it be the sun's distorting rays that make that
Grass greener?
As a deep blue wave, I shall wash those shores
But never flood it.
   Deborah Ballinger

Deborah Ballinger, a civil servant, was born in Birmingham
in 1969. This is her first published piece of work.

I Am Not A Number: Damned Statistics

Button-holed
by a relentless
researcher,
with pointed pencil,
gripping a clipboard, and
urging me
to spare a moment,
to answer a few
questions.

Close-up, faltering,
pencil hovering
over various categories;

I await her
tactful probing,
diplomatic approaches,
as her efforts
endeavour
to pigeon-hole me.
   C. A. Baldock

Carol Baldock, from the Wirral was born in 1950. A mature
student with three children. Runner up in 1990 Liverpool's
F.O.C.; recently joined the Pilgrims Poets. Published in
magazines and anthologies. Enjoys writing and humour; hates
bills and exams.

They Shall Not Grow Old

Again I hear the fine old words, and once again I ponder.
Thinking back to other days, when as a boy,
They always made me wonder.
Young men in droves, gave up life's joys.
To die in tatters yonder.

The Somme again we must recall, down all the bitter years.
The young men's blood, became the mud.
The pools a nation's tears.
How brave they were, no man a dud
My heart, their spirit sears.

Through shot and shell and cruel barbed wire.
They soldiered on, as they were bid.
They offered their flesh, to feed the fire.
Till smoke the carnage hid.
The God of War, fed his desire.

The Hearts at home, were sorely tried.
What for, such price be paid?
For what end so many died?
At who's door, can blame be laid?
When Heaven's Angels cried.

When silence came to battered field
The shattered men, all scattered lay.
Our nation's youth, no earthly shield.
Were 'dust to dust, and clay to clay'.
A harvest of red poppies yield.
   John Young

John Young was born in Burntisland, Fifeshire in 1920. He
is a retired ship constructor and now lives in Dublin. He has
written poems and short stories, also novels and expects to
publish them in due course.

Hallowed Ground

Through the looming gates we walk
with tears that cloud our deepest thoughts,
amongst the sombre stones of death,
utter not one silent breath,

a tranquil place, that feels so calm,
where life and death walk arm in arm,
where greatest peace surrounds my soul,
to this my broken heart console,

and though this place is so serene,
it's always in my darkest dreams,
a place where former lives are laid,
and friendships lost are then remade,

where mortal shells are laid to rest
after living life's great test,
but peace surrounds this holy place,
the stepping stone to god's great grace.
   David Kerrick

David Kerrick is a 27 year old nursing assistant who is still
quite a novice in the art of writing poetry but who has a
lot more to offer given time.

Soul Searching

Reality, that faithless stray
has turned away from me today
Is this madness or invention?
Every heartbeat takes me down
to deeper levels, tighter tension
where I reach the darker ground
Here the world tilts on it's axis
and everything is slanted strange
voices boom in shrill crescendo
familiar faces seem to change

Soft earth that springs beneath my feet
holds trees that whisper to conspire
with whipping wind and rolling wheat
to lift my sinking spirit higher
As birds take off in startled flight
soaring to where the sunset glows
I am bathed in gentle light
and communion with creation flows

Colossal sky of turquiose splendour
luminous field of molten gold
As dying sun bleeds in surrender
I breathe the glowing ether cold
Glorious planet, amorphous mother
in your essence I refresh
my cloistered spirit clothed in garb
of flesh that cannot bear the press
from love that fills my soul to bursting
This heart's too narrow to contain
such emotion ever thirsting
for its peace from joyous pain
    Gloria Allan

Gloria Allan has lived in Nottinghamshire for 30 years, she
writes poetry and short stories and is a member of Mansfield
Writers' Workshop.

Battle Ready

All effort has been for this moment,
Poised
On the brink of battle.

Every stretched sinew,
Each shining shield and muscle,
Corned and calloused hands,
Sharpened sword and eye.

Dancers
For the Dance of Death.
All for now;
Now!
The great moment of standing still in the Universe.
Perfection of an untroubled heart
With no more thought of you or I.
Of you or your sword
Of me or my sword.
Of skill,
Of life,
Of kill
Or death.
All is emptiness!
Then devoid even of emptiness.

And out of this infinite emptiness
Comes the most wondrous
Unfoldment of doing.
   Tony Bonning

Tony Bonning lives near Biggar in the Scottish borders where
he runs 'The Mythological Bookshop'. He is also the founder
of 'The Festival Of Myth, Legend and Folklore' held in
Edinburgh last year (1991).

That's What Got Me

She had a face like a squashed up raisin
Don't think I didn't like her, though...
I followed her for
What?
About an hour,
Dogging her
In and out the shops.
The little slut.
I mean,
I really liked the green
Umbrella she swung.
You know how it is -
By hook or by crook.

Well, they keep me pretty quiet.
Don't think I don't like it here.
There's a pot of shrunken heads -
Lilacs. Purple things that hang
Together like dried peas
In a white pot.
It's too small for the window.

Lying low
I see her face sometimes,
Slatted like venetian blinds gone wrong,
Eyes linked like tiny hand-cuffs.

I cried when they sliced a tomato.

The quiet's too noisy.
You know how it is...
Ghosts on haste;

Every bedspring in blossom,
And the walls
Always
Changing shape.

I followed her a long time
Before she clocked me.
She checked her watch
About a million times.
I watched her.
The clock in the window said four -
That's how I reckoned an hour.

It wasn't raining.
That's what got me
In the end.
She swung the green umbrella.
She'd never be my friend.

They slice the tomato
With a fruit knife,
Ridges on the edge.
It makes me cry.

She never saw me
Till the end.
I licked her raisin face
And her screamful of ecstasy
Finished me.
  B. Porter

Beth Porter is an actress, writer and drama producer who
co-starred in 'Rock Follies', 'The Men's Room' and Woody
Allen's 'Love and Death.' She's the London Editor of 'The
Film Journal', and is BBC Television Drama Series Script
Executive in charge of development.

In England

In the Autumn when winds scatter
the last of the summer fruit on the ground
Berries gleam brightly in every country lane.
In spite of first frosts there are flowers to be found

Whilst every evening plans and schemes are made
                              for winter once again.
There's woodsmoke and fireworks and children's laughter
Christmas golden with benevolence of loving and giving.
Whilst the last roses blossom with a hope for ever after.
A better way for everyone for life and living.
Individual freedom with kindness and humanity.
Merging with the hope of all mankind.
Staying undefeated with reason and reality
bringing and comforting a peace balm to the mind.
    J. L. Louse

Joan Lucille Louse, a pensioner, lives with her son in Walton.
She has worked in production and later, in an old people's
home. She has written a great deal of poetry although this
is her first attempt at publication.

To Travel in Hope

Up at dawn to beat the crowds,
Scan the lightening skies for clouds.
Tell the wife today's the day
You're finally going to get away.

Check the papers for a site
Load the car and grab a bite.
Drive into the countryside
(But you're not going for the ride).

Taking books and records too;
Assorted clothing; and a few
Old knick-knacks from the garden shed;
An Austin tyre with half it's tread.

And finally an old paste table
To put them on, so you are able
To do your best to fill a pail
With money at a car boot sale.
    Peter Dunn

Peter Dunn has lived in variety of places and has had a variety of vocations. Currently a Northampton lawyer, his published articles cover such interests as books, chess and murder. Other interests are bridge, Mensa and Glenys.

Unity

I cast my cares, my spirit doth leap,
And into the net my catch I keep.
The river is deep, my life is long
But now I have it's constant song.
The music of life plays unseen strings,
A harmony pervades it's bounty brings.
Spellbound am I for surely I see
Purely and simply - a unity.
   Ros Needham

Ros Needham is a watercolour artist and walker, her favourite places being the Dales and the Lake District. She has recently developed her natural love of poetry, illustrating her observations of nature in all it's moods.

Please, Let There Be

Words cannot recapture
The Memories of Time,
Experiences of Long-ago.
The sad, the joy sublime.
But ah, the quiet of the night
Just before you go to sleep,
When nostalgia calls your name once more,
And back those memories creep.
They melt into your drifting mind
And accompany your dreams
And you meet once more those folk long gone,
Or so it often seems.
Then awakening at morning
Feeling just a little sad,

After dreaming of a grandmother,
A dog, or dear old dad.
Do you, like me, unashamedly,
Close your eyes and pray...
...'Please let there be a heaven
Where we can meet again one day?'
   Douglas A. W. Box

Douglas Box lives in Horley, Surrey. He has recently had
a favourite poem called 'When' published in the Wildlife
Guardian and is hoping to get his collection of poetry for
children published.

In Search of Peace

A sea wind eats the early flames
That sear our weather-beaten towns.
We learn the dead-and-buried names
Of tearways who drove like clowns.
Was this why brave young pilots gave
Their lives with Churchill's fearless few
For this, we screamed at deafened graves
From Iraq, back, to Waterloo.
Was this why Mrs Thatcher cried
The war she lost within our shores
In search of peace our forebears died,
Their hearts last beat in foreign wars.
Then who'll lead England from within?
The Queen's relations feast and play,
The Church and clergy preach of sin;
John Major fears election day.
The army's dreaming overseas,
Police they stalk the DPP.;
Great towns and cities on their knees,
The least protected you and me.
   Joe Rogers

Joe Rogers lives with his wife Kathleen, and the youngest of their five children in Cheshire. He is a member of the Creative Writing Workshop, Rotunda Community College, Liverpool; and the Theatre Playwrites Workshop, Liverpool University.

Senses

We take for granted many things
Especially gifts most dear
Like listening how a blackbird sings
Thank goodness for the ear.

To see the sunshine at it's best
High in the clear blue skies
This wondrous gift that we possess
Thank goodness for our eyes

To smell the scent of new mown hay
The fragrance of a rose
And new aroma's everyday
Thank goodness for the nose

To touch a babes unwrinkled skin
Such smoothness, how it lingers
And fasten closed the safety pin
Thank God for thumbs and fingers

To eat our bread and drink our wine
And not let fresh fruits waste
How wonderful to sit and dine
Thank goodness we have taste

While thinking of our senses rare
Some might say one is missing
It's used most widely everywhere
Called plainly - intuition.
    Jon Snow

Jon Snow lives in Eastwood, Nottinghamshire, he gets his inspiration from that same countryside and community. His ambition is to write a novel.

Each Morning Now

Each morning now has a little nip in the air
Evening's getting shorter with less time to stop and stare
The trees are changing colour and what a heavenly sight to
                                                        see
What a joy to live in England, there is no other place for
                                                        me
People sporting hats and gloves wrapped up nice and warm
Thinking maybe the weekend will be the last to cut the lawn
Rough weather forecast with strong winds, gales and
                                    blustery showers
Take heart our florists are there in abundance to save us
                                    lovely flowers.
Maybe winter 1991 will have just a hint of snow, hanging
                            in cascades from each tree.
Children playing with snowballs and sleighs tumbling around
                            and laughing with glee.
Winter is now almost upon us, year being 1991
And for most all of our lovely birds their last summer song
                                    has been sung
Just a hint of mist and fog appearing each morning
Nature is such a wonderful, exciting and mysterious thing
The trees now have that beautiful tint of gold, pale yellow
                                and deep burgundy
Oh what a wondrous sight for all to see
Cobwebs glinting through the sunshine gently nestling in the
                                            hedgerows
And in the fields little groups of noisy crows.
Squirrels are busy gathering their winter store
Up and down the trees and still they find more
Today is dull with large clouds drifting low across the sky
Just visible an aeroplane appears and one thinks from where
                                        and why

It is darker now and the rain softly pitter pats against the
                                                window pane
In the distance I hear the joyous sound of a large steam
train
The wind is gaining momentum and gushes into trees,
                        buildings and everything in it's wake
At times it is quite frightening, when the building starts to
                                                        shake
But hark the wind is softening and a faint blue sky emerges
Soon there will be brilliant sunshine and little ones will be
                                skipping along the verges.

    Dorothy Stevens

To a Snowdrop

Flower of simplicity,
Like a knight of old,
Fighting your way
Through rain and cold,
Living for centuries
Your tale to tell.
First to come and first to go,
Little white bell.
Call as you ring,
Winter is turning
Into sweet spring.

    Joy Michie

Joy Michie was born in Putney, London in 1914. A retired
librarian now living in Herne Bay, Kent with her husband,
she enjoys reading, writing and lace making.

The Hypnotist

Oh! Mr West the hypnotist
Help me if thou can'st
Rid me of this debilitating
All-pervading angst.

My paranoia is a problem,
The kleptomania too,
So give me that old hypno stuff
That only you can do.
Fix me with your steely gaze
As on the couch I lay
Clear my mind of useless clutter
So my problems fade away.
Calm the whirlpool of my mind
And while your at it, why
Not make me see that I don't need
All the alcohol I buy.
Let me hail a bright tomorrow
Free from forty fags a day
And the marijuana too
I'd like to throw away,
And while I'm in this deepest trance
Could I ask you, please
To cure my toe-nail biting
So I can the say Jees -
Us Christ I'm free at last
From the shackles and the chains
And with a mind as clear as crystal
I can start it all again.
    V. F. Clark

V. F. Clark is a 56 year old property manager who has lived
in Cambridge for thirty years and has just started writing
poetry.

The Mighty Machine

Men with their engines, criss-crossing continents
On concrete roads, scars on the world
This need for speed, driven by greed
Polluting the air, dropping their litter.

Clogging up cities, choking the countryside
They call it progress, how wrong can they be
The word is rape and only rape
Apply the brakes, slow down and stop.

Smell the roses, touch a new-born babies face
Feel the warmth of the summer sun
As you wonder, stop and ponder
On man's desecration of this beautiful world
  M. Martin

Mary Martin has always lived in Devon, now retired from
a hectic business life, she has time to devote herself to
writing short articles and poems, many of which have been
published.

Rapunzel

You didn't consider,
you weavers of tales,
that I, in climbing the golden ladder,
would needs make sacrifice,
Look how...
She tantalised with her light-voiced song,
tortured with her weeping
and I, compelled by your telling
of my tale as a hero,
followed the notes I heard,
the signs I perceived -
and did you weavers know of her pretence?
Weavers consider this now;
Rapunzel let free
laughed at my fate -
locked me in her tower.
Look how she mocks...
  Jill Pickering

Jill Pickering .is a published poet - now. Born in Lancashire in 1967, she teaches English in Kenilworth and travels; by sea, land, air.... and magic carpet.

Good Neighbour

I'm not one for gossip,
But it must be plain to see
The antics and the carry on
From the one next door to me.

Happened to clean my windows,
In the bedroom next to hers
And goodness me the racket
Put my duster in reverse.

Wondered what was happening,
Behind that stout front door
Only natural really
As I've met her type before

Don't you be long I begged him,
As he went to fix the nail
I wonder if he noticed
That she was far from frail.

No, I'm not one for gossip,
Specially about my Jack
I'll just carry on my dusting
And hope he soon comes back.
    Joan Hughes

Joan Hughes lives on Merseyside, she writes short stories and is currently working on her first novel.

In the Time it Takes

Days...

In the time it takes a leaf to fall
fingers close around a tender moment
shyness aches and pain
such visible pain is held as precious.

Days like ours...

In the time it takes for rain to fall
words echo within our weakened hearts
silence seeps and nothing
not even hope intrudes.

Days like ours carry burdens...

In the time it takes a tear to fall
light fades behind this hidden peace
darkness creeps and blindly
shapes strain against their gravity.

Days like ours carry burdens of separate weightlessness.
    A. J. Green

A. J. Green was born in Liverpool in 1962. He has several
vices and even fewer virtues. It is rumoured that one day
his life will amount to something but he is not taking bets.

Grandmother's Picture

I remember a picture on my grandmother's wall
Of seas lashing rocks that stood very tall
A storm battered ship tossed about by those waves
Was it carrying a treasure, or transporting slaves?
The mast was in half, the sails hanging low
The wheel was unmanned oh! where did he go?

My eyes drifted down to an object afloat
upstretched arms of a figure clinging to the hull of a boat
In the corner of the picture was a bright light
Sending out rays in the dark of the night
A warning for ships that sailed the great seas
Beware of the peril, from those rocks you must flee
The artist revealed a scene that was grave
A tribute to those who ride the tempest are brave.
   Maureen Goodenough

Maureen Goodenough is married with four children and ten
grandchildren. A keen sea-angler, she enjoys writing poetry.
She lives at Fair Oak in Hampshire and works full time for
an electronics company.

Guilty?

The hand inserts - then, the victim
Small, unwanted, defenceless with no blame;
This is not the whole truth of it;
For why should we pay with our lives
For one moments forgetfulness.

Is it a crime to love, but not love
The result of the first's haste?
Whether a crime or not, who are we
Who have never lived with unborn child
To judge and pass sentence?

Come child of mine, who was born
Through two but left with one
Into my arms and melt the guilt away.
   Sally Gemmell

Sally Gemmell lives in Fife. She started writing poetry at
the age of 16 and this is her first publication.

The Stillness Reigns Supreme

There's a moment of time in every day
When stillness reigns supreme
Like the stillness that before the rain
Comes late upon the scene
Or when the buzz stops and the pollen is drawn
From a flower by a wandering bee
When a horse drinks and it's muzzle is dipped
Into the nearby stream.
When the weather is hot and the swifts will scream
With an electrifying burst of speed
But just before they swerve, they glide
And the stillness reigns supreme
   Simpson Miller

Simpson Miller, a livestock auctioneer and valuer, lives in
Crickhowell, Powys. He would one day like to publish a
collection.

Shop of Dreams

Do I see what I think I see?
I can't believe I do,
That shop was not there yesterday,
And yet, it isn't new.

The tinkling of oriental chimes.
Signals the door is open wide.
A smell of incense on the air,
I have to go inside.

Before the window I hesitate,
This place is not for me.
It's for exotic, exciting types
The sort I'd like to be.

Joss sticks, candles, Tarot cards,
A cornucopia of jewellery.
Enamelled in vibrant colours
And work in silver filigree.

Nothing in there is ordinary,
Not like me and I make a vow -
I will become a customer,
Someday, sometime, somehow.
    Julie Glover

Julie Glover is married to a farmer and is the mother of
two children. This is her first published poem.

Mirrored Truth

Stranger in the mirror,
A reflection,
Showing imperfections,
In the face,
I saw as ageless,
Within my mind.

Stranger in the mirror,
Sighing,
Sadly denying,
Refusing to believe,
The evidence,
Of slow decline.

Stranger in the mirror,
A reflection,
Of introspection,
Mourning my lost youth,
In the quicksilver,
River of time.
    D. Hale

D. Hale wrote features and articles for the Glasgow magazine 'Streets Ahead'. She now spends most of her time writing poetry; and is currently researching material for her first novel.

Miss Fidelia Crossley Crossley

Miss Fidelia Crossley Crossley
In your little Comper Swift,
Defying the force of gravity
With thrust and drag and lift

Though I'm vague as to where you're going,
And don't know from whence you came,
Fidelia Crossley Crossley
I admire you for your name

I wish that I could fly with you,
No prospect could be sweeter,
What a pity that your Comper Swift
Is just a single seater
   Peter Hull

Peter Hull, now retired, has spent much of his life as an RAF flying instructor and then as secretary of the Vintage Sports Car Club. He has had several books on motoring published.

Idol

We are so alike on the spiritual plane,
and yet we have a different name.
Reserved, aloof and rather shy
annoyed by others when they pry.
We hate the noise and love seclusion
alone with our thoughts and sad illusions.
Analysing at every chance,
feeling the victim of circumstance.

Our marriages failed we thought were for good
but hoped in the future we would be loved.
Your timid and fragile, old for your years
and yet quite a joker behind all those tears.
I'm small and I paint whenever I can
a portrait of you my favourite man.
Suppose we met what would I say
people like me you meet every day.
A brief hello, a smile, a frown
another face in another town.
    B. J. Harrison

Barbara Harrison was born in Bradford, she is a retired
shorthand typist and amateur artist.

A Poem About Dying

Death is as real as life portends to be,
Obsequious: the image is to me
Latent, boring, pessimistic
Old dreams and favours anachronistic
The passage open to me:
Death is as real as life portends to be.

Death is as warm as my wrists are cold,
Sheer white-black, obtusely bold
Frailty from omnipotence, dominance
My absence shows my prominence
Finger-fist tight to hold:
Death is as warm as my wrists are cold.

Senses dim and furrow brim-grim,
The invisible boy is dead; 'Y'know him'
That one, his passage to sin
Collected, unprotected,
Eyes close and tears thin:
Senses dim amd furrow brim-grin.

Death is as real as life portends to be:
As warm as my wrists are cold,
Senses dim and furrow brim-grin,
Numb as ice from limb to chin,
Power is dominance is tolerance
And I have lost no prominence.
  Daniel James

Daniel James is a 16 year old student in his final year of
'A' levels. He hopes to study English at university and
currently lives in Norwich.

Our Garden

There is a place, a place for us
Away from all the city fuss
A seat beneath a shady tree
A place of peace for you and me
To sit when we are feeling low
With flowers that are all aglow
And water rippling peacefully
Where fishes swim so silently
There's no such place I hear you say
Oh yes there is, not far away
And what is more, I beg your pardon
I'm speaking of our lovely garden.
  Alfred Harris

Alfred Harris was born in London in 1939. He loves the
country and gardening, which is now his living. His poems
are inspired by his family and life in general.

The Eye of a Needle

Surrounded by an army of sand
A lizard skids past.
Is this my dream or anothers?
For I am without camel.

Not a cigarette or the beast
Just a means of escape
That or a life amidst
A land forever thirsty.

I can't remember arriving
Just a sudden claustrophobia
A burning upon my brow
Weary of confusion.

Equipped with nothing
But a brain
I know not how to use
Fate will smother me.

Whether it's sand,
Or a serpents cruel kiss
I will never use cowardice
For without a camel I will ride.
   Angeline Hamilton

Angeline Hamilton is a seventeen year old who is studying
for her 'A' levels as well as writing poetry in her spare
time.

Parting

They said...you know it's for the best
They said...it's only right
They said...she was so peaceful
when she passed away that night

But memories now is all we have
Of good times all gone by
They said...but that's important
and should fill us with joy

They said...an awful lot of things
when we put her in the ground
But words can't change the feelings
Of sadness that we've found
   Arthur Howe

Arthur Howe was born in Coventry in 1931 and still lives
there. Graduated from Warwick University as a mature
student in 1985, he now works as a driving instructor.

The Model

She poses for the camera
looking into the lens
She moves around so that
he can get natural shots.
Her bleached blond hair
Shines in the lights
The rays are centered on her body
Her face has been made up
by the make up girl
The model's lips of red, pout.
Her chin lifts then she turns
her head to the side.
Another days work
another picture in the magazines
The lights are centred on her body
The outline of her shapely body
Breasts exposed.
No clothes.
Agencies take most of the money
The model, keeps on to earn a living
and revels in the thought
of being on the shelves

looked at
Could be famous for fifteen minutes
Exploitation
Dirty old man
Dirty old men.
The model happy in
Ignorance.
Fades away as she gets older
Is not needed
put on the shelf.
Looks and body lined and floppy
Left feeling rejected, depressed
Thoughts of the past relived
Now appear.
Now appear.
Trying to recreate the past
Is laughed at
pictures in the box, she keeps in her room.
   Debbie Hobbs

Debbie Hobbs was born in Cambridgeshire and now lives in Brighton. She has been writing poetry for fourteen years.

Don't Bother to Look

You sit there with your head in a book
Life goes around you, don't bother to look.
The book holds you more and I'm second place.
You didn't notice the book on my face?

I read, too, in a nonchalant way
But at least still hear what you have to say.
I will stop and listen, not too engrossed
You are more important, to me the most.

The book will wait, but my life won't
Time will run out, the book will go on.
Can't we recapture the love we shared
Or is it too late, our life is blurred.

No more talking as we used to do, has the rot set in?
It's not too late
You could take my hand and say something
You could first talk and look.

But that would be stupid, we're too old for that
In silence we sit, me with my thoughts
And you with your book.
Am I realistic - don't bother to look.

You've made me wonder what I saw in you
Where in that dashing youth I knew
When did you lose your vitality
And why, oh why, didn't it happen to me?

Sit there and read and in every nook,
I'll guarantee,
You won't bother to look.
    J. Hurst

Jan Hurst has reached retirement officially but refuses to
recognise it. Her motto is 'Keep going - keep growing'. She
lives in North Wales.

Plain Sailing

Run my hand through the water,
the tack needs to alter
just twenty degrees to the North.
The wind is due West,
my life's full of zest and
I'm happily sailing on course.
Don't miss work or the bus
or the problems and fuss,
I'm just living my life on the sea.
Just sailing and fishing
and sometimes just wishing
it's how my life always could be.
The sun's shining down

-138-

there's no problems of town,
it's so quiet and peaceful out here.
There are birds in the sky
and no question why
I should have anything ever to fear.
No one to question me
What is my destiny?
Who cares? I'm just heading North.
Sun, rain, snow or hail,
if there's wind in my sail
I'll keep happily sailing on course...
   Jackie Gibbs

Jackie Gibbs is a graphic designer and lives in Orpington, Kent. She enjoys writing poetry and is currently writing a book.

The Choice

Today it's hard to make the choice
Should I stay quiet - or use my voice
So much to say, so much to do,
but should I stand still or run on through?
I could stop a fight,
I could save a life,
I might stop a war,
I could pull a knife.
There's causes to fight,
There's rallies to attend,
Politicians to rebel against,
Rights to defend.
Should I stay back in the crowd,
or the front of the queue?
Should I stand still
or run on through?
   Rosemarie Garcia

Rosemarie Garcia was born in Hackney, East London. She writes poetry as a hobby and has written articles for magazines. She works in London's Guildhall Legal Office.

The Wanderer's Return

The lamp post at the corner,
That sheds it's friendly glow,
Over the old familiar streets,
That once I used to know.

The church that stood upon the hill,
The bells that used to ring,
The tiny little choir boys,
How sweet they used to sing.

The village green, so fresh and sweet,
Where the children used to play,
And that old wooden summer house,
Upon a rainy day.

All the dear familiar things,
Sweep over me anew,
I wonder, shall I turn a street,
And catch a sight of you.

The fragrant scent of roses,
Fills my heart with pain,
Brings me back those long lost days,
When you were mine again.

It's heaven to return to it,
And feast my eyes once more
On all the dear forgotten things,
That once I knew before.
   D. M. Gibbs

Dorothy Gibbs, born in Montreal, has been writing poetry
and short stories for many years. She lives in Romford,
Essex, alone with her Labrador. Has had five poems
published.

Parting

It's been a long time since we were together
though we often meet.
The thread is broken
and we call across the cavern in an affort to retrieve
the happiness we had.
In all the chaos of the weeks
When we fought blindly over trivial things
something slipped away.
And now it is too late.
So we smile and talk our mouths all motions
while my soul quietly crumbles.
   Henrietta Forrest

Henrietta Forrest lives in Somerset with her two children.
As well as writing poetry she is also trying her hand at
illustration.

Inner Peace

Be at one with the earth
Your life, your land and place of your birth.
Keep peace and tranquillity between all fellow beings
Never become engrossed in evil, hatred feelings.
Everyone is given the right to live
And every single person has something to give.
Life is all about giving and taking,
And keeping friends, not making and breaking.
Believe in yourself and your dreams will come true
And all through life remember you're you.
   L. J. Fairhurst

Lisa Fairhurst is seventeen years old and studying for her 'A' levels. She hopes to take English Literature at college in September, and this is her first published poem.

Rape of an Old Lady

It seems I have lain here
since the beginning of time -
old and brown and furrowed.
Wind and rain have beaten my skin
the colour of tanned leather.
Fingers of early morning sun
have crept into my cold heart
and warmed me into life.

Countless times have men
caressed me, worshipped me,
used me and left me
naked to the elements.
Each new man secretly, silently
warmed the life within me
and brought it forth.
My fecundity was endless.

Then he came -
ripped away my mantle of green
and left me bleeding in the sun.
My silent scream was carried
on a skylark's wing,
and hung in the air.

Too soon I showed the fulness of his seed
Here in the old brown hills
I could not hide my shame.
Amid the muted hues
I advertise his progeny -
a blanket of acid-yellow rape.
   Judith Elton

Judith Elton keeps goats, hens and horses as a hobby, and teaches primary school children in the Quantock Hills in Somerset.

Heart Bypass

There's a bypass around my heart
keeping emotional traffic away,
protecting my city centre
from the smog of a lovers day.

There's a ringroad you will travel
but you just cannot get near
to the streets where all my dreams walk
all the accident's ther've been here.

Perhaps a ghastly oversight
but there's nowhere you can park,
the traffic lights are always 'go'
and poor streetlighting means it's dark.

There's no tourist guide provided
I quite frankly think it's wise
you travel other highways
like my every sign implies.
   Simon French

Simon French was born in Worthing and has performed his 'Noisy Poetry Show' in Sussex theatres. In December 1991 he presented morning shows for Worthing's first radio station as part of the national charity organisation 'Radio Cracker'.

A Dilemma of Youth

Her big blue eyes were full of trust,
Beautiful bairn, now only dust;
To hold this child who came from lust,
I'd give my life: I've been unjust.

My gift from God had his consent,
Moulded from earth and the child meant
To live full life: be competent;
Sacred is life, despite advent.

I feel regret, I am distraught,
Desire the babe, the life God wrought,
That I might love, cherish, support,
Yet her untimely death I brought.

The day the woman took to hold
My darling child I had her sold
Distaste I felt: sorrow untold;
My rights were gone, in place was gold.

I often brood, I'm kept awake,
As I recall my big mistake,
When from my arms I let her take
The child I'd born: leaving heartache.

Neglect, abuse, her soul laid bare;
Compounded acts in public glare
Passed unheeded: seemed not to care;
No love or care, lived in nightmare.

Through ether surf, my soul will jet
When call is made, then Maker met:
He may forgive, but can't forget
And soon I know I'll pay my debt.

(When fifteen years of age, the lady was raped, and
circumstances obliged her to exchange the resulting child
for money. Paid by a couple unable to produce children, they
soon found the substitute unacceptable and with time became
uncaring, eventually resorting to hideous abuse prematurely
ending the young life.)
  W. E. Fisher

W. E. Fisher was born in Hucknall, Notts., but now lives in Yorkshire. He has had many poems published and hopes to publish his own collection shortly.

Fragile Earth

The World is slowly dying
Poisoned sea, polluted air.
Clouds of acid-rain are crying
Killing forests, trees grow bare.

No fish will swim the oceans wide
When precious plankton dies
Killed off by oil upon the tide
Where washed up sewage lies.

No birds will trill or swallows dive
Where toxic-fumes rise high.
No honey bees within the hive,
Or gentle butterfly.

The earth was once so green and chaste
But now a dumping ground
For every kind of nuclear waste
That in the world is found.

The many resources that we use
And take for granted every day
Without a thought of their abuse
Will dwindle fast away.

For the sake of all the human race
Each one of us must try
To make the earth a better place
Or our world will surely die.
    Joyce English

Joyce English is a retired telephonist born in County
Durham. She writes poetry for her own pleasure and hopes
to have some of them published.

Slaughterhouse Meat

I can't wait for it to leave, I hate all
That flesh sagging, falling in the wrong
Direction, like slaughterhouse meat
Waiting for inspection.

Short skirts and fat thighs, sunny skies,
MacDonalds children wearing what's advertised
Slob parents in rainbow suits buying
Sugar mountains and cholesterol takeaway
Why didn't it rain today!

Shiny chrome comes in and out, trolleys
End up beside an old trout. Roy
Orbison's sunglasses, golden oldies
With bus passes direct their heap
To a check-out girl that's half-asleep

Polluted breath, munches his treeburger
His disney kids have air in their feet
Ten spoonfuls of sugar and a mystic
Pizza to eat

I hate the sun, am I the only one? I don't
Think I like people much, either money
Swallows up the till as they fumble with
Cash cards and cheques, you would think
They were making a will!

His breasts are bigger than hers the
Flab he no longer fights, into his
Feast of chocolate he bites, I wonder
Who those trousers were meant to fit?
He sweats like a suspect, and wipes
Out every last bit.
   Stuart McMillan

Stuart McMillan is unemployed, enjoys writing and would like
to make a career out of it.